Many Mountains Moving

PRINT ANNUAL

Vol. VII, No. 1, 2006

(the seventeenth issue)

A
LITERARY
JOURNAL
OF
DIVERSE
CONTEMPORARY
VOICES

www.mmminc.org

*A*RTS *FOR A S*USTAINABLE *C*IVILIZATION

The Day When Mountains Move

Akiko Yosano

The day when mountains move has come.

Though I say this, nobody believes me.

Mountains sleep only for a little while

That once have been active in flames.

But even if you forgot it,

Just believe, people,

That all the women who slept

Now awake and move.

This poem was originally published in 1911 in Seitō ("Blue Stocking"), a Japanese literary magazine. It was reprinted from *The Burning Heart: Women Poets of Japan* (translated and edited by Kenneth Rexroth and Ikuko Atsumi, Seabury Press, 1977).

§ § § § § § § § § § § § § § § § § § § §

This seventeenth issue and first print annual anthology of *Many Mountains Moving* is dedicated to our founding editor/publisher, Naomi Horii, whose vision and wisdom made all of this possible since 1994. We continually wish her only the best since she left *Many Mountains Moving* due to different kinds of priorities at the end of 2004.

We must also thank the past poetry editors, Debra Bokur and Alissa Norton, the past nonfiction editor, Steven Church, and the past technical manager, Jim Uba, for their tremendous work for so many years. Thanks also to the many other people who enabled *Many Mountains Moving* to transform itself again.

§ § § § § § § § § § § § § § § § § § § §

Directors
Jeffery Bahr, Jeffrey Ethan Lee and *Erik Nilsen*

Poetry Editors
Jeffrey Ethan Lee and *Erik Nilsen*

Fiction Editor
David Rozgonyi

Contributing Editors
Jeffery Bahr, Barbara Ellen Sorensen and *Bryan Roth*

Cover Photos
Joseph Sorrentino and *Sylvia Glassman*

Logo Design
Craig Hansen

Design
Jeffrey Ethan Lee

Assistant Editors
Malinda Miller and *Erin Viel*

Interns
James Kerley, Doug Baker and *Peter Derk*

ISSN: 1080-6474; ISBN 10: 1-886976-19-8 ~ ISBN 13: 978-1-886976-19-1
Published annually by MANY MOUNTAINS MOVING, Inc.,
a 501(c)(3) nonprofit organization. First North American Serial Rights. ©
MANY MOUNTAINS MOVING 2006.
Many Mountains Moving
549 Rider Ridge Drive, Longmont, CO 80501, USA
Indexed by *The American Humanities Index* (Albany, NY; Whitston Publishing Co.)
& *The Index of American Periodical Verse* (Lanham, MD: Scarecrow Press).

●

Many Mountains Moving
now takes submissions
online at www.mmminc.org.
Visit the site for details of
the new system that can save
natural resources, time, energy
and money.

This publisher is a proud member of

COUNCIL OF LITERARY MAGAZINES & PRESSES
w w w . c l m p . o r g

We would like to thank the many friends and supporters whose contributions and subscriptions have made this print anthology possible. Special thanks are due to the following: *Anonymous, Jeffery Bahr, Jan Carroll, Patrick Lawler, Jeffrey Ethan Lee, Malinda Miller, Erik Nilsen, Barbara Sorensen, Sonya Unrein* and *Erin Viel.*

We would also like to thank organizational donors whose past or present support enabled Many Mountains Moving, Inc. to conduct literary salons, literary festivals and writing workshops: Boulder County Arts Alliance, an agency of the Boulder City Council, The Community Foundation Serving Boulder County, Boulder Museum of Contemporary Art, the Scientific and Cultural Facilities District (SCFD), the Boulder Public Library, St. John's Episcopal Church in Boulder, The Tattered Cover Bookstore (Denver), and The Boulder Bookstore.

Many Mountains Moving, Inc. is also grateful for marketing support from the **Council of Literary Magazines and Presses** and from **Small Press Distribution** (http://www.spdbooks.org/).

Finally, many thanks to our readers and contributors, who are dedicated to opening an exchange among cultures through art and literature.

Many Mountains Moving, Inc. is a 501(c)(3) nonprofit organization that publishes this literary journal and poetry books through the Many Mountains Moving Press imprint. If you work for an institution or organization that supports literature and the arts and wish to make a tax-deductible donation, or know of any individuals who wish to make a contribution, please ask them to contact us at Many Mountains Moving through our website: http://www.mmminc.org.

CONTENTS

Volume VII   *2006 Print Annual*

§ §

FICTION

§ §

POETRY

SELECTIONS FROM THE POETRY BOOK CONTEST WINNER
AND SOME FINALISTS:

§ §

NONFICTION

§ §

PHOTOGRAPHY

§ §

CONTRIBUTOR NOTES   268

*Congratulations to the first MMM Flash Fiction Contest
Winner, the Honorable Mentions, and the Finalists!*

Winner:
Jeff Fearnside, "Nuclear Toughskins"
(published here and online at www.mmminc.org)

Honorable Mentions:
Karen F. Groves, "Buyer Be Wary"
Andrew McNabb, "Extraordinary Whiteness"

The top Flash Fiction finalists:
Jenny Lentz, "Natural"
John E. Branseum, "Babies"
William Donnelly, "This is Not a Ghost Story"
Deb R. Lewis, "Waiting at One End of Time"
Jennifer L. Schultz, "Murder"
Sandra Maddux-Creech, "Soul Cats on the EL"

And many thanks to our judge, Thaddeus Rutkowski, author of
Roughhouse (Kaya Books, 1999) and *Tetched* (Behler Publications, 2005).
http://www.thaddeusrutkowski.com/

All of the entries were judged anonymously.

Nuclear Toughskins

My dad built a bomb shelter in our backyard the year I was born, between the Berlin Wall and the Cuban Missile Crisis, but it soon became a neglected cave of concrete and canned peaches over which my best friend Johnny Lynn and I ran barefoot and ice-cream sticky on hot summer days, or stalked fireflies at night, or threw our heads back and stalked stars, my dad standing over us tracing the flight of what we couldn't see, saying, *They're up there, boys, looking down on us as we speak, that's why it's a race to the moon, everything's a race.* Then muttering *godless heathens* he'd light a Salem and suddenly say, *Wave to them hi!* and we'd all wave except Johnny Lynn, who'd give the Reds the bird, though you couldn't tell, he was so tan and his gesture just part of the night. My arms were tan, too, but my legs were as pale as the powdered milk my mom would sneak from our cave when we ran out of whole, because no one in our family wore shorts, it wasn't allowed, something in the Bible supported this—Sodom and Gomorra, I was led to believe. But Johnny Lynn went to the same church as we did and was as dark as an Indian from the thighs down, and my parents never said he was going to hell, though I knew he swore and gave the Reds the bird and old Mr. Franklin, too, at the five and dime, not because I ever saw it but because my friend said so. I wanted Indian thighs and grass-stained knees but was afraid I'd be turned into a pillar of salt or destroyed by fire. Not even Armstrong's one small step could change my fear—it took the three channels on our TV, Mark Spitz and his seven golds, the forbidden rock on my transistor radio, and Skylab, which I imagined was manned by Major Tom, and by the summer I was twelve I couldn't wait to take my protein pills and put my helmet on, so one day I cut up a brand-new pair of Toughskins jeans. It wasn't easy, because new was when they were best, like Dacron armor, but I figured if you could make a trampoline out of them, then they would make good shorts. The only thing is, I couldn't cut them with my school scissors or even my Scout knife; I had to sneak my mom's sewing scissors out of her basket, and I still had a hard time, especially with the reinforced knees, but when I was finished they were even cooler than Johnny Lynn's. And for one glorious afternoon I ran with the freedom of one who lived free, who felt the heat of sunburned shinbones yet also impossible light and air rustling through downy hair like a breeze through curtains before a thunderstorm, ran as an equal with my friend. We danced and taunted the sky where we knew Salyut lay hidden godless behind clouds, *Look, Reds, look at us, see how we live in America!* until my mom heard and chased Johnny Lynn away before scolding me inside and stripping me to my briefs, fretting about what to do with my sin. She didn't tell me to wait until my father got home like she usually did but instead scolded and fretted and then finally made me dig a hole in the garden, where she deposited my new Toughskins shorts like they were a full diaper, covered them up, and said not to tell my father unless I wanted a red bottom.

They're buried there still, I guarantee it, have outlasted Vietnam, the Olympic boycott, the Cold War, Star Wars. They were probably just getting broken in when the Berlin Wall fell. Someday somebody will dig them up, long after we've finished the arms race and visited Mars, long after perestroika, the Second Coming, the two-thousand-year reign of the Prince of Peace my mom still says is right around the corner.

Love, Miranda

Eddie Martin's car smells like salty fish. When I slide in, he shuts my door and goes around to the driver's side. Under the yellow streetlight he looks like a quarterback walking onto the field for the final play. In the car beside me, his eyes jump from my bare knees— I'm wearing a mini skirt; guys like mini skirts—to my breasts and then my smile. His lips jerk into a quick grin, then he concentrates on the steering wheel, the radio, the road. Anything but me.

Eddie's the eighth guy I've dated in the past two months, since I started my sophomore year of high school. I'm working my way through St. Cecilia's boys. I don't like them. I like parts of them: Tom's hair was clean and wavy and smelled like almonds. Stuart wore a pretty gold necklace. What I like about Eddie Martin is his hands. They're wide and slow, with thick fingers. If his hands were to build a house, they'd build it one board at a time, and the house would never fall down. If I'm going to give up my virginity, I might as well give it to a guy who's careful with his hands.

Since Miranda left at the end of summer I've been trying to lose my virginity. Before the dates, while I put on mascara and lip gloss, I go through the pep talk. No big deal. Girls sleep with guys every day. Love isn't necessary. Then he picks me up, we go to a movie, I make the right moves. He gets excited and at the last minute I chicken out. I get goose bumps or a cramp in my leg. I say wait no I'm sorry I just can't.

I'm lucky. None of them have forced it. But I'm still a virgin; I've still only slept with girls. I mean Miranda.

Eddie takes me to a movie and then we drive to the lake. He eases into a parking spot and kills the engine. The lights on the water are brassy gold.

"Awesome view," I say. "It reminds me of trumpets." Miranda would've said *I know!*

But Eddie stares out the window and scrunches his forehead. His fingers drum the wheel. Better get the show on the road. I slide over to touch his collar. He has a sharp smell: cologne, vinegar, sweat. I put my face to his neck and kiss it, watching myself from outside.

I'm an easy first base. He pushes me into the vinyl and gets to second. His hands aren't slow after all. Third. I don't think of anything. I empty my head. It's easy to look over Eddie's shoulder at the gold water, when he says, *Can I?* Easy to say yes.

I get home and take a bath—it's true what they say about bleeding your first time. All I want to do is call her. I want to tell her about Eddie, how I gritted my teeth the whole time and felt ripped open. How I still taste his tongue in my mouth.

Instead of calling I get under the covers and re-read her letter. My light, she says, I miss you. I wish I was there with you, I would read you stories and we could write stories together and teach each other new things and wonder and guess and laugh and stay up all night to watch sunrise. We'd go fishing, pick raspberries, make pie. Your soul fits mine and mine yours and so forever I am truly, Yours, Miranda.

She writes once a week and leaves messages on the machine. I stopped returning her calls two months ago, after my first date. But she hasn't given up. I write back, and put my letters in a box at the back of my closet, with hers.

Miranda has crazy red hair flying all around her face. And freckles all over her body. One summer at our private spot by the lake I counted them. She said it was like counting stars. But I got two-hundred-twenty-six on her left arm and then when anyone mentioned freckles, she quoted me.

Every June for the past twelve years, Miranda has ridden the Amtrak out here from Topeka, Kansas to stay with her Aunt Barbara, three houses down from mine. I don't remember meeting Miranda, but my mother says we were friends the minute she and Barbara put us in the same sandbox twelve years ago. She looks a little different, thinner or taller or more hair, every June when she steps off the train, but we never have to warm up. Right away we're talking and giggling like no time has passed. Separated at birth, my mother jokes.

Last summer we talked about boys.

"The girls in my class are all obsessed with boys," I complained.

"My class too. It's disgusting." Miranda made a face.

"My growth must be stunted. I'm not interested."

"Simple," she said. "Girls rule." We laughed. "I'd rather be with a girl any day."

"I'd rather be with you."

We wrote letters all year. We sent pressed flowers and butterfly wings and love sonnets copied out of old books. I didn't tell anyone—just nursed my crush through a long winter and spring. In June Miranda was prettier than ever. And in July she kissed me.

Mr. Gregorian saw us. He'd set up a pinball machine at the back of his soda shop, and when Miranda and I finished our milkshakes, we slid off the bar stools and went to play. After a couple rounds I got the high score and she kissed me. Not on the cheek, like I told my mom. We were excited, laughing, and Miranda screamed and gave me a quick kiss. Congratulations. Then she came back and did it again, slower. Her lips were warm. I felt like I'd grown wings and they were lifting me off the floor.

Mr. Gregorian stood behind the counter. He didn't say a word to Miranda and me, but his stare burned my shoulders as we walked out. When I got home, my mother was sitting on our living room couch.

"Kelly, I just had a call from Frank Gregorian."

Compared with the bright summer afternoon, our house was cool and dark. I stood with my hand on the doorknob, waiting for my eyes to adjust.

"He said you were kissing someone in his store. A girl, he said. Do you want to tell me about this?"

"It wasn't a kiss, mom." I started to make out her eyes and the soft flyaway strands of her hair. "I mean, she kissed me—"

"Who kissed you?"

"Miranda."

"Oh?" My mother loves Miranda. Every June when she arrives from Kansas, Mom makes hamburgers and strawberry cheesecake, Miranda's favorite dinner.

"It wasn't a kiss. I mean, it was on the cheek. I got the high score in pinball. She congratulated me. Why do I have to justify everything?"

"I'm sorry, honey. Frank made it sound like—"

"Well, it wasn't." I took the stairs two at a time, shut the door to my room and stood against it, my heart beating high and fast in my throat.

The next evening Miranda and I waded through the tall grass behind her aunt's house toward the old barn. Its open door looked like a mouth belting out a long, strong note. Walking beside Miranda, I stared at the lake-blue sky and found the first star.

"Whenever you see one star, you can always find another," Miranda pointed.

"There you go, reading my mind again," I said.

"Your mind, my mind, what's the difference?" The grass rustled against our hips.

The barn smelled like straw and wet wood and animal sweat. Bridles hung along the far wall. We climbed the ladder to the hayloft and sat in the wide window, looking out over the rooftops, our feet dangling far above the ground.

"Mr. Gregorian saw us," I said. "By the pinball machine. He called my mom."

"He did?"

"I told her it was you, and it was just on the cheek."

She brought her knees up and rested her chin. "I kissed you because I wanted to."

My chest tightened. I looked from the dark field to Miranda's face, familiar as my own reflection, but bright with an expression I'd never seen. As if she'd thrown off a mask and become herself. She loved me.

"I wouldn't mind if you did it again," I said.

She leaned over and rested her head on my shoulder. The stars kept coming out, one little pin of light after another. After a while she kissed my neck, then the soft spot below my ear. I wasn't afraid like I am with St. Cecilia's boys. I turned my face toward hers and we touched, forehead to forehead.

The hay tickled at first. We spread our coats out and lay on them, close together, kissing and then not kissing, feeling each other's bodies with our fingertips. I touched her mouth and felt that she was smiling, and it made me laugh.

When we left the barn, the night air was cool, the stars thick, the Milky Way a white sash rippling through the sky.

Miranda and I were lovers for two months, and we kept it secret. At the Amtrak station we held each other for a long time, promised to write and both cried on our separate ways home.

The first day of school, I walked into Algebra and Jenny Rodman waved from across the room. Jenny pretends to be best friends with everyone. When I sat in the desk beside hers, she touched my hand and smiled. "Kelly, how are you?"

"Great," I said. "How about you?"

"I spent the summer in France with Todd's family." She and Todd have been going together since sixth grade, and wedding plans are in the works. "It was fabulous. What did you do?"

I looked at Jenny's gold earrings, her pretty hair and long eyelashes.

"I fell in love."

Jenny lifted one of her thin eyebrows. "Anyone I know?"

"No."

"Did you go all the way?" she whispered. Her grin was contagious.

"You could say that," I said.

Mrs. Nelson bustled in and class started. Jenny passed me a note: *Does this enchanting lover have a name?*

I fingered the paper. It was true love, my first. I had to tell someone. I wrote *Miranda* and passed the paper over. Jenny scribbled and flung it back onto my desk. *A girl?*

I stared at her and nodded. Jenny looked as though she'd swallowed something rancid. At the bell she brushed past me without a word.

That afternoon, people hissed *homo, queer,* in the halls as I passed.

Nobody looked me in the eye. At three o'clock when I left the school grounds and headed across the street, some guy yelled, "Look out! Lesbo crossing!"

I wheeled around. Kids milled all over the school steps and lawns. Anyone could have said it. All of them must have heard.

"If Miranda calls, tell her I'm not here," I told my mother that night. "I need to study."

"Already? The first day of school?"

"You wanted me at a college prep school," I snapped. I sat on my bed reading American History and bit my tongue when the phone rang.

Queer, faggot, dyke. It went on for a week. I walked across the baseball field at lunch and sat against the chain link fence. I tore up blades of grass, watched the clouds and talked to Miranda. The answer was silence. Someone painted my locker: *Fist me, I'm gay.*

Monday of the second week, I picked the burliest guy in first period and went over to his desk.

"Hi," I said. "I'm Kelly."

"John." His thick forehead made a shadow over his eyes.

"John," I said, kneeling down and crossing my arms on top of his desk. "You don't have a girlfriend, do you?" We shook our heads together. I asked him out to a movie. He said sure.

John. Bruce, Philip, Jeremy, Stuart, Tom. Eddie Martin. I pick the ones who wear cologne, whose voices have changed. In the girls' locker room I tell stories: how the guys look without T-shirts, how they kiss. In Study Hall I lean over my notebook and compose love poems, careful not to write her name.

The morning after Eddie, I nod off in English class. When everyone's cleared out, I go over to Mr. De La Rosa's desk and ask about the assignment. It's a paper on *Catcher in the Rye.*

"Is anything wrong, Kelly?" he says. "You seem preoccupied." Mr. De La Rosa and I were friends last year. I helped him clean the blackboards while we talked about Shakespeare and Thomas Hardy. "Does it have to do with the rumors going around school?"

"What rumors?"

"I know you too well to believe this," he says. "But rumor has it, you're sleeping with different boys."

It's working. Suddenly I miss Miranda so badly my chest aches.

"I'm not interested in boys, Mr. D."

He searches my face. "What's going on, Kelly? You've changed. Did something happen over the summer?"

I look at the paperweight on Mr. De La Rosa's desk: streaks of color floating in glass, like frozen eels. If I told him, he'd keep my story to himself.

"Yeah," I say. "I met someone." I think of the spray of freckles on Miranda's pale cheeks.

"You're in love." He smiles. "That's wonderful, Kelly. What's his name?"

I stare at my teacher. The air in his classroom is too hot to breathe.

"You don't have to tell me," he says. "Love makes me crazy too. But it's worth waiting for, Kelly. The real thing's worth waiting for." He winks. "I'll keep your secret."

I cross the paved courtyard under trees rustling in the afternoon wind. Everyone has gone home and the yard is deserted. I pass through the empty halls with their quiet rows of lockers. Somebody painted my locker again. Slut.

I run. Down the brick steps, across the sidewalk. Block after block, with Miranda's voice in my head.

"You're going to forget me," she said one night. Her eyes were sad. Her voice with the rhythm of my feet. Forget me.

I stop at a curb where traffic roars. I'm panting. Air cuts through my ribs. My hair lifts from my shoulders with every passing car. A city bus lumbers toward me, rocking side to side, its face silver and blind. Just one step down. Easy. I breathe and lift my right foot and the bus goes by and I fall back, stumbling.

Car after car rushes past and none of the drivers look at me.

"How could I forget?" I told her. "My heart's made of you."

I see her standing on a sidewalk in Kansas, alone like me. There's no one to talk to. She's thinking it would be easy to step down, throw her life in front of a bus.

Across the street at the drugstore there is a phone booth. I approach the curb again and run. Drivers lean on their horns and brakes screech. I make it to the drugstore, the phone, and grab the receiver. It is cool in my hand. I dial the number I know by heart.

Chords

He rolled over onto his elbow, reached his arm across her breast and kissed her forehead as she hummed some obscure Polka tune. She seemed better lately, the late night wakings and weepings alone in the bathroom had stopped about a week ago. But the dreams were still there: *I dreamt I was on a roller-coaster with a friend.*

It was Saturday, that time just before dawn when they woke up on days they didn't work, their bodies caught in the time signature of first shift jobs. She pushed herself up out of the covers and leaned back against the wall, reached a hand down to his hair. He could barely see her in the opaque room, waited for her to keep speaking, fought falling back into the warm currents he had drifted out of.

"It was one of those giant coasters like at Cedar Point. You sit in the seat and know it is going to be a long ride. As it started I turned to look at my friend Lisa—she was my best friend in twelfth grade—I haven't seen her in over eight years. She wasn't sitting in the car beside me, she was behind me. She started calling. I turned—she didn't have a seatbelt and we were reaching the top of the incline. Everyone was starting to gasp and I could barely reach behind me, she was starting to scream and then we plunged and I was grasping for her hands and then we turned upside down and she started to slip. I wasn't scared for myself at all. I was scared I was going to lose her."

"What happened then," he asked.

"I woke."

~

The year her grandfather died she began to play the accordion.

In the mornings she'd slide out from beside her husband, from beneath the quilt her grandmother had stitched, put on a pair of worn sweats and a long shirt to cover the chill of early spring. She walked over the tiled floor, and he heard her peeing in the near dark bathroom. She squatted half-hunched so as not to touch the cold seat. She never flushed so as not to wake him. He heard her tiptoe over the cool

23

linoleum hallway, socks shush shushing over the living room carpet, the clicks and locks unclacking as she opened the large trunk that held the white and black accordion. His ears held the slight wheeze as she lifted the squeeze-box to her chest. He heard her lean into the first few notes as her fingers found the keys and the pages flipped as she scanned the few simple songs she was learning. And then she would sit there in silence—he didn't know why she did that. Sometimes for many minutes. At first he thought she'd fallen off to sleep. Or was she praying? And then she would begin, the first few notes like round words, then small sentences.

The accordion had been a gift from her grandfather to her father when he was a little boy. But her Dziadzia hadn't been the one to teach her father to press the keys and make the box crescendo. The old man had told her once, "You can't learn to play from someone you live with. Love: it gets in the way." And there was something of love in the words her father had said to her that day, patting the accordion, the great black box that wheezed the way he would sometimes, lighting a cigarette, then coughing into his balled fist.

"One day you will make the room twirl."

"Sixty years and what does it get you," her Dziadzia said to her. The steel plant, then the mill along the lake. Then those many years working for the city, driving the red siren'd plows, pushing the piling snow, as the wind swept off the lake in great silent sheets.

~

Stephen, go to your room and practice, he would yell at me. Her father: *I must have been about five when he had me start playing.* He looked at the boy, the one his daughter had brought home for almost a year to their new two-story Colonial north of the old east side neighborhood. He was getting used to this scruffy kid, getting used to the color of his light eyes and his Irish name. He liked how the boy never touched his daughter in front of him. He had seen them walking down the wide sidewalks by the dirty bay holding hands. They walked with a foot between them, not leaning against each other. There was something in the boy that made him keep his mouth shut. Not like the others: The one he had chased out with a sideways spit curse. The one whom he had spoken too harshly to with a poker in his fist. He liked how this boy had nodded his head and asked how to do the steps when the old man had been playing in the yard that afternoon, watched how the boy took his oldest daughter's hands and copied her steps, spinning 1-2-3 across the lawn. This one was ok, the father told himself. He liked how the boy listened, only every now and then lifting a hand to brush his slightly too long blonde hair out of his eyes. He forgave the boy his torn blue jeans and his T-shirts. "He listens," the father told her mother once in the kitchen, her mother dusted in flour rolling pirogies. "He listens not like a kid listening to his girlfriend's father. He listens as if he's trying to hear something in what everyone says. I mean he really listens."

Her mother turned and smiled at him. He laughed, "Not like me, huh Sophie." And the father grabbed her mother by her thick waist and pulled her to him, hummed the tune of a made-up Oberek in her ear. She reached a floured hand back to touch his face.

~

"When I was a girl," she told him, "When I was a girl I used to dream of spiders."

He was bending over to fix the neighbor boy's bike. "They were everywhere," she said. "The house was covered in white webs and I could be pulling at them, over and over, pulling at them, entangled, calling for my sisters, my brother, my father, my grandfather."

He lifted his head, staring up at her in the driveway. Behind her head the sun, her face dark in silhouette. She was trying to tell him something more than the words she was saying. He knew this, and sometimes he could hear what that something more was, something he could catch, like a spider catching a fly, and hold it, and drink it down to its dregs. And when he did this he knew he had done well—like how his mother, those nights when she lost control, would come into his room sobbing and turn on his desk light and lean and tell him about every little thing at her office—filing, phone calls made, her father, about burning his cuff ironing, and he knew something was wrong with her, but he knew it was something below the words, and if he listened close enough, everything would be all right with her, and she would see he had caught her words and what was beneath her words, and she would kiss him on the forehead and go to bed and he could go back to sleep.

~

My grandfather is dead.

The day of the wake it was snowing. He wore his best white shirt. He parked three blocks away from the home on 26th Street, in the old Polish neighborhood where almost everyone now spoke Spanish. There were candles in every window and rosaries in every pocket. They played Salsa at the Warsaw Café. In Kossuth Park Dominican men sat smoking cigarettes, flipping dominos. Old aunts in babushkas sold homemade pickles at the corner bodega, right beside trays of meat-pies and red beans. "Some things are still the same as when Dziadzia grew up," he told her as they sat in the chairs by the coat room. "The language is different, but the churches are still packed. No priest is going to go out of business here." The uncles in their baggy blue suits were all there, so many he lost count. The aunts didn't wail. He thought, that's something different. No black-netted grieving like the new old women in this neighborhood. Polish women make it go. The five daughters greeted everyone, consoled more than were consoled. His girl's three sisters came and sat with him. Lisa, her youngest put her head on his shoulder. She feels it more, he thought. She came back with a ten-year-old girl who looked red eyed, had been crying, a cousin, and they took her hand and went up to the casket. Her Dziadzia was laid out in a white ruffled shirt, a blue jacket. Same one he wore twenty years to church. They knelt with the little girl named Ruby between them and he felt her tiny hand begin to shake. He closed his eyes. Then they were back standing. Her father was saying something to him and he was trying to listen. There was a prayer said by the Priest who was a cousin. He lost her again, talked to an aunt. Her father didn't cry. Her mother looked embarrassed that she might weep, he felt ashamed he saw. He wanted to put his arm around her but only touched her shoulder. He didn't even know if that was the right thing.

~

She began taking lessons every week at Pulaski Brothers over on the East Side, the same neighborhood her grandfather grew up. *Mr. Pulaski taught my father and now he'll teach me.* She bent down and pressed her red painted nails onto the gold keys. A single shaft of sunlight fell through the hanging begonia. He followed her eyes out at the window as she watched the traffic race down 10th Street, watched the spring's opening branches gently sway. He became aware of the cool floor on his feet and the hair on his arms. She was playing something without a melody as if just warming up was a kind of searching. Then her eyes returned to the kitchen table and she turned the page and began to play "Batter Up," the child's song everyone learns to play no matter what instrument.

"I played saxophone as a kid," he told her. They were up late again, the sounds of traffic shushing through the cold early spring rain. "My father was a jazz freak remember, I wanted to be John Coltrane," he said.

"I wanted to be Lenny Gomulka," she laughed. "The greatest Polkateer of all."

~

He wasn't sure which night she started talking to herself. At first he simply thought she was talking in her sleep. She did that sometimes. *Missy don't wear that it's mine... Sorry I don't have the exact change...* common phrases from the day, or something strange and oblique, like *No, No eggplant purple, like that girl's handbag by the bus stop.*

He remembered his grandfather, the smell of pipe tobacco on his breath, the brush of his forearm against his cheek. His grandfather liked to hum, doing whatever he was doing. He hummed old Irish songs, work songs, and every now and then an old standard like "Misty" or "Sentimental Mood." The house was always filled with his humming. He met her the year his grandfather had died: fourteen summers ago.

Does the story of that matter?

He didn't know why he asked it. He was trying to make sense. She was fingering the golden keys, her hair in her face, the windows open and

27

the warm wind blowing in through the begonia on the window ledge.

He began to listen to Polka that year. "Do you remember," he was saying this to her now, "the story of us." She was beginning to play, the notes pulling her away from him, not pulling her out the window where her eyes were gazing—pulling her into *fields outside of Warsaw Station her great-grandmother bending to tie her brown boot her jasha eating the kasha kishka where is Papa the snow piling up across the sidestreets singed with Polish old babushka'd women carrying pillows sacks of vegetables over their stooped shoulders sweet pickles and sausage casing the black earth the black soot of the steel mill the black snow her grandfather telling her about the black snow when the mill flames burned the sky her grandfather walking booted in the black snow press the keys press the skies the rising riding the plumes of ashes the plumes of red petals across the snow the cold wind black suited her father playing the accordion for hours for days playing his grief and then he put it down her hands found the keys piano lessons recalled she pressed and wheezed I am going to take lessons she announced at dinner the drives back to the old neighborhood I can't hear him I am forgetting the teacher began at the beginning she thought back to his beginning he is a child he is humming in Polish eating a pickle his knee is bleeding slur the note lift your knees pig knuckles and pirogues the blessed bowing in Saint Hedwig's the black Madonna blessing the just baked bread.*

He wasn't there when she opened her eyes. She let the accordion sink into her thighs, feeling the weight of it, like a large child, as if she held her grandfather as a child. He was so light, she thought those last days as she guided him from the bed to the chair. *If I am not careful he will blow away.*

"When I was a girl," she said, " I would hide in the closet until someone realized I wasn't there."

She was drinking a glass of green tea on the back porch.

Who is she talking to, he thought, as he watched her through the kitchen screen. "My mother would grow frantic and begin to stutter my name over and over. One time I did leave the house and they found me almost a half mile away. I had packed a peanut butter sandwich and a sweet pickle wrapped in plastic. I am headed to Dziadzia's house because *he knows who I am,* I told them. The policeman who found me, ate half the pickle I offered him. What is your favorite animal at the zoo, he asked me. The zebra, I said, because its stripes make it invisible."

~

What is this, she asked?

"I didn't know how to give her the accordion. Whether to just leave it for her to find or to present it formally, with a big ribbon, maybe even a corny concerned speech, 'I've been worried about you. I know things have been hard on you.'"

"Hard on her?" Stymie said at the 8th Street bar. "Man, alls she does is squeeze that thing all night and day."

Stymie, his best friend since they used to cut high school together, smoking under the bleachers or hitching a ride to the 10th Street Diner where they slurped eggs and ignored Pepo's questions, "Why you boys never in school, you gonna be bums." Stymie who once drop kicked a girl's pet pig because she turned him down. "That kid's problems are a courtroom's worth," his old man gruffed. But Stymie turned into the straightest dude when he found Laura, or Larushka as they called her, Russian girl who slapped him, pulled his face and cursed him in Russian. He sat in the Orthodox Church, in the purple light, and learned to pray. Stymie whose mother drank herself to death, lifted his glass, and uttered, "She'll play herself into a Polka band in Buffalo and where will you be?"

I'll be her biggest fan.

He had used the secret money he'd saved for the last two years, folding the $20 bills into tiny spirals he kept in the silver piggy bank he'd had since childhood. Where would you want to go if you could go anywhere he asked her all that year. *Poland, Paris, Peru.* Whatever was on the television, some far away landscape, not just a place to sit and forget the dayshifts, the too-many hours working.

"He wants it back," she had said last week. "My father says I can't take his accordion with me anymore. He misses it in the house. What am I going to do?"

She had been crying at the dining room table for a long time before he came home, her face scarred with blue mascara, blue mascara over the pile of bills and yellow plate, blue mascara on her thick hands.

He sat at the table, fingered a pile of bills, "Play over there, you should be over there more anyways. Let them hear you. Play over there after work."

After work now for two months she would go home to her parents' house and sit on a straight wood chair in the living room, where she learned to sight read as a child, and pull out the great accordion, slightly too big for her still near-girl hands, and she would lean into the songs her grandfather once played: Obereks, waltzes, childhood tunes leading her slowly into the fast Polkas, honky style I will play one day, she said, Chicago style, my own band. Same as every Polish girl he teased her.

On the west side music shop he found a woman's size accordion. "Works well," Antonio told him, ran a hand through his half bald gray hair. "This kid's mother's from the neighborhood, he brought it in after she died, I said why don't you play the thing, and he just laughed, all that wack wack wack shit kids listen to these days. Have you ever heard Benny Maroni slide into Amour with this behind him? Shame now, you want it? Pay me a little now and I hold it and you pick it up when you can. You try it, I don't know, squeeze it and press, do you think I know? Trombone I played when I was in school. Everyone wanted to play the trombone back then, be in a big band. Here I wipe it off, look at the shine. Kid said it was in the case in the attic, said he never heard it, didn't even know his old lady could play."

~

"I bought you a woman's accordion." She just sat looking at it. He didn't want to cry in front of her.

That day he had walked to the great cemetery and sat on the old man's stone. "Her grandfather's over there, Pop," he had whispered, "She's leaving me, you see. When you left, I became an orphan. It was like when Mom left, but worse. Because I never told you but I knew when Mom left you would never leave me. It's all these spaces Pop, all these spaces around us, in the air, over there. See that woman, I see her walking here most every day, she sits in front of the plate with her name on it. Imagine doing that? I want to ask her if she wants to be down there beside him. That kind of loss. I was so small but I remember watching you after mom died. I remember more you watching me. You never left me, Pop. She came to me the year you left and her hands brought me back to the rain against my bare head. Now I have to give something back to her, Pop. I don't know how but I need to bring her back to the dirt and the street and the children playing in the park. Pop, I don't know how to get there."

~

"When I was a girl," she said to him, "I used to pick dandelions in the park. I called them Sun-flowers. I thought that was their name. I would pop off their heads. One day my mother caught me eating them, said they were dirty weeds and who knows if dogs pissed there. I'd sneak them into my pockets after that, eat them when we got home. When I pooped, there were all these tiny, golden petals swirling between my legs."

~

He woke up to find her not beside him. He could hear her in the bathroom weeping—or was she laughing? The little keys of her voice echoing through the long hallway.

~

He drove home hours before she got back from her shift at the Laundromat. She came home smelling like just washed wind. The job was hot and harsh but for that alone he longed she'd keep it. She would crush herself into his arms. It had been so long since she had done that. Usually she walked in, showered, said a few words, and went to bed or smoked out on the porch. "I need to be alone," became an unsaid thing. Her voice echoing into itself. Her voice a half-held thought. Her voice that stuttered along wherever he wasn't. A half note not uttered.

He didn't smile, didn't dare to wince. *Baby,* he wanted to say, but held his breath. She nearly tripped over the black box positioned nonchalant against the CD case, half thinking maybe it was her father's, half forgetting where she was. She bent, looked up at him, bent. She touched the black leather surface, then said, "What's....?" He thought then he would cry. She leaned the case down on the cream colored carpet, held it with both hands, laid it down like a cradle. She undid the silver buckles, snapped them, and breathed. He didn't want to look, touched his hand to his chin, then gave into a small grin. She wasn't watching, then she opened the case slow as the yawn he struggled through, wiped his eyes. He saw the worn lining as she slid the velvet slip cover off the black instrument, ran her right hand along its smooth shine. Then she reached both hands down and around, lifted it slow, balancing it, pulled it towards her chest, arms into straps, hands on key, the wheeze and breath of it. The slight exhale of notes, an off-key chord. He could barely contain the breath he wanted to let into noise. Her brilliant shine.

Then nothing. Nothing. Was it broke? Was something wrong with it? Was she pressing the keys? He went to stand. He didn't know, couldn't. She unstrapped the bellows.

She looked at him then. She saw what she hadn't been able to for so long—his eyes pale as rain, the black tattoo he got when he was fifteen and they were hitch-hiking to the punk shows in Cleveland. Lemmy was that kid's name who inked you, wasn't it, she asked him one night before her grandfather had died. Yeah Lemmy, he had answered. They had been sitting up late on the back porch, drinking, talking small.

Polish kid with a lisp.

He looked down at the barbed line along his bicep. She loved him so much then, Did he know that?

~

"When I was a girl," she said, "I would sing in the choir at Saint Hedwig's. My mother first brought me to Sister Agnieska when I was nine. She said, you have been touched by Gabriel. She had found me in

32

the back singing a Donny Osmond song to myself. She thought it was
the radio. I loved to be near Sister Agnieska in her blue habit, surrounded by the icons of Our Lady. She taught me Lily of the Valley, and then
the Latin. The sounds filled me with fields and rivers. My father would
come home from the factory and every evening he joked, 'Teach me
a new tune,' just to hear me sing. I sang every Friday after dinner. Me
who had been invisible. My Dziadzia was the one who said, 'Give her
the piano.' He was the one who paid my lessons. In high school when
we ran away, when I stopped, it broke something inside him.

"He was dying, and I was sitting at his bed. He was wind thin and
my face was made of water. He said, 'play for me, play.' I couldn't even
make a chord. All I could do was finger a few off-key notes.

"But he put his hand on my leg, and said, 'Good, good.'"

Many Mountains Moving Press is pleased to announce

the 3rd Poetry Book Contest Winner:

Silkie by Anne-Marie Cusac

forthcoming in 2007

Anne-Marie Cusac's poetry has appeared in *Poetry*, *Iowa Review*, *TriQuarterly*, *The American Scholar*, *The Madison Review*, and is forthcoming from *Crab Orchard Review*. Her first poetry book, *The Mean Days* (2001) was published by Tia Chucha Press and won the Posner Book Award from the Council for Wisconsin Writers. A recipient of a Wallace Stegner Fellowship at Stanford University and a Wisconsin Arts Board Individual Artist's grant, Cusac was for ten years an editor and investigative reporter for *The Progressive* magazine. Her investigative reporting there won several awards, including the prestigious George Polk Award. As of fall 2006, she is a professor in Communication at Roosevelt University and a contributing writer for *The Progressive*.

Runner-Up:
Cynthia Arrieu-King, *People are Tiny in Paintings of China*
Honorable Mention:
Veronica Patterson, *Close*
Finalists:
Sheila Black, *Love/Iraq*
Lisa Lewis, *Vivisect*
Renato Rosaldo, *Clockwise Modern*

●

Many thanks to our final judge, Patrick Lawler, author of the 2nd MMM Press prize winner, *Feeding the Fear of the Earth*.

Semifinalists:
Charles Atkinson, *Thumb Against the Sky*
Michelle Bitting, *Communion*
Lorna Blake, *Permanent Address*
Laurie Blauner, *The Age of Ventriloquism*
Dana Curtis, *Camera Stellata*
Pat Falk, *Crazy Jane*
Daniel Lusk, *The Bull on the Roof*
Adela Najarro, *The Swarming Background*
Chad Sweeney, *Salt Plain and Other Stories*
Dona Stein, *Evergreen*

wild enough

There were stories
    about girls wild enough,
        one in particular, Dulsie
            in her pale green halter, the faint
            shadows round her nipples, the way (we all noticed)
            they changed in the school air conditioning,

the school yard cigarette
    between her lips.
        Those lips
            could do anything: the scornful
            smile, the sneer, the break
            into warmth no one ever expected.

She could
    start screaming
        and still hold a cigarette
            in the corner of her mouth. When she
            breathed it in, her eyelids
            drooped, and she looked to the side, as if

she whom we thought
    so known, so physical,
        so summed
            in the calf muscles flexing, the wonderful
            body stretching from the arched
            foot through the fingers, all of her was lost

the moment
>> she tasted
>>>> the cigarette,

>>>>>> and we didn't know her.
>>>>>> Girls like her, wild enough
>>>>>> to sleep alone on the beach,

not once for kicks,
>> but again and again.
>>>> The seals

>>>>>> can spot a girl like that, can see
>>>>>> the light her body throws off, and everything
>>>>>> we miss about her body.

There were stories
>> of how she woke
>>>> in the dark

>>>>>> and the sound of lapping waves. The tide
>>>>>> crept almost to her feet but didn't
>>>>>> touch her, and the body

six inches from hers
>> wept its heat.
>>>> It was the one

>>>>>> she needed, the sand
>>>>>> giving under her shoulders, right there.
>>>>>> Later, she woke again, tide long out.

The body that
    had what?
        Loved her?

            was gone. In the shallows
            paddled a harbor seal,
            watching her the way they watch us.

silkie song

She flames like a window at evening
her hair the color of late sunset
so low and molten it drips into the water.

I shake myself hard
and follow the coldest current
until I see the mackerel
running for open water,

stomachs fat with the heat they've eaten,
gills streaming light like notched lanterns.

I pound my tail. I catch one
and another, another, another.
I tear into their bodies
until I cramp with belly fire
the color of her hair.

theft

Late at night, she separates her body,
      leaves him dozing, hitches up
her cutoffs, yanks down the T-shirt,
      forgets her shoes, runs for home.
The piled sealskin trips her, and she gasps,
      fur spiking her calf
wet, oiled, sand-crusted. His smell,
      but stronger, submerges her, waves of it lapping,
and her insides lurch with desire
      for what, in the darkness, she can't make out lying there
until, thinking *of him of him,* she gathers
      the folds of skin to her chest. The smell appalls her,
its raw, watery meatiness. Her cheek flinches
      at the clammy underside. But by now she has found
she can't put it down.
      It weighs as much as a bagged six-pack.
In the streetlight, fur pricks
      and glitters. Voracious, she drinks
the smell, beastly, nearly human.
      This, she thinks, *is what we want.*

IN THE PORTRAIT OF SOLITUDE

I'd met several girls who so reminded me of myself, I was embarrassed
to look at them, their questionable hair, or let one girl know she appeared
in my dream as some version of me, and directed me to lead her, instead
of walking on her own. It was as if I had looked straight into a mirror
and instead of seeing only myself, I saw another person so similar,
light went through the window and got confused
as to whom should be illuminated in the portrait of solitude. But then,
we thought the better of contrivance, or I did, and twins and quadrads
and everyone started to become lean in the vexing glass, where
like it or not, we were swept together.

RED NOBODY

Then we entered the lily
built white on a red carpet
—Lorine Niedecker "Club 26"

A flat-lining patient blows up the scale of what bystanders
can take. Black gun-shot face.

I could offer: This is bracing,

admirable, a saintly adventure. Or: nurses—eyes rolling—
exchange sighs.

The nurses think her time is up— ask
why do we keep shocking the heart?

——

Near Death, a slide down an electric slope on which one feels
singular,
lone—

down the rivulet sides, it's too hard to return the gaze
on one's back.

This fall in the dark.

The nurse marks it with small red flags and flares
so the patient might know which walls
to bounce
against on the
way down.

We scrawled a red aloha alongside carabina'd
lines:

aloha, aloha
Cave.

————

Hands crossed, pressing compressions.

A woman stopped at a red light, staring.

It's not that compassion fatigues, knowing who can't be saved,
or what makes no difference.

Our doctor doesn't believe he'll raise the dead with wires and burns—
he's lived this freight for years; unwraps chocolates, flips through
sales circulars.

Jokes. With
a memory full of holes,
one gets repetitive.

Patient with hair
fluffed as down. Soon she's gone.

————

A body still needs a few people to lift it
with a sheet.

The sheet lessens its weight.
The lifters only feel
a twinge of foresight.

Death,
despite the red drugs, the IV drip rates,

is the older—
may even think, like the old do in their wheelchairs,

how amusing,
to move
without moving.

Survival

I traced the scar above your lip, the peculiar motions
of peculiar history

You fell off a scooter on a cobbled street
You told me this and, of course, I imagined

the apartment house yellowing in the sun, the crumbs
of plaster, the dent in the marble stair

the balcony of wrought iron and inside

the piano with its dusting of lace, the gold-rimmed
vase for the flowers

a brass platter on the table, the ordinary fruit:
apples, bananas, a peach from the mountains where

they bloom just below the line of the snow,
the burning sky above

where the air is thin, the women grow dry,
toothless, having long buried their weary husbands

You at eight, riding with your brother

None of it real. All in a breath. The cigarette you held
to my lips, around us the flow and eddy

of the boulevards clogged with cars, not so different
from the air than the veins of an immense body

cells multiplying, consuming,
sloughed off, away—where to?

From that distance who would know your story,
your particular exile or that at eighteen

you had worked as a radio communicator near Abadan,
the last outpost of one of the centuries'

many half-forgotten wars. They were boys, the men
who served under you

at night they put their hands between their legs,
crouched over like dogs

cried out in their sleep, uncontrollable
as urinating

This was your life after. You buttoned my fur coat
to the collar. We walked down the streets

in the Northern European rain, chill, still,
smoke rising from our mouths

and at night in the camp bed, our limbs crushing each other's,
we slept badly. We slept well

We drank coffee so hot it scalded our tongues,
devoured the fresh bread, something to believe in

the hard crust and the soft steam inside
so much like the idea of flesh

soft, rich and sweet with the hard wheat
harvested from golden fields.

The dead boys hung about your shoulders,
their childish arms, the backs of

their necks. When you kissed me they
were there, those furred young

bodies with their smell of milk. How
carelessly they were scattered

over the nameless landscapes. Nothing there but
the odd smoke rising, the buried wires

sudden flares. *Nothing we would not do.*

How it might have happened

1.

The bomb was meant for you. You had secret lives of which we knew nothing.
If you could build a cloud, you could rule the world. The men in the car
littered the pavement with their cigarettes, waiting. One scratched a mosquito
bite on his neck.

2.

The bomb was not a bomb, it was a stick of simple dynamite. The men,
breathing heavily, ran around the corner.

One said: *Too bad about the car.*

3.

How do such bombs get built? I prefer to think of the before. Men in rented
        apartments
with concrete balconies. A woman under a veil crossing the road
below whose hand grips the hand of a child. A boy, six or seven, with cropped
        hair and
unreadable eyes.

The concrete. That feels real. The look of concrete in sun. A sensation a
painter might work years to capture. Laying down each layer in heavy
impasto, looking for the perfect mix of glitter and dead rock.

4.

The bomb was made by someone who believed. They heard the
noise. They never looked to see what was left or if

the bomb was meant for you, which it wasn't. There was an under-minister or

47

a police chief, an American official of dubious provenance. You walked down
     that street
every day on your lunch break.

Why? Because of the almond trees. Because there was a swallow's nest
somewhere. Because of the girl in the coffee shop whose
hips reminded you of mine.

5.

No. You had not thought of me in years. When you had it
was like a wing cutting the air, the movement created all-but-
imperceptible. You thought of me and did not know what you were thinking.

I came to you as chime, a flavor of the wind.

6.

You were in love. You walked down that street precisely because
it was fractionally less crowded than the others. A silent suburban corner:

Almond trees, parked cars, sidewalks stippled with the shadows of buildings
and gateways.

You rehearsed conversations in your head.

When you reached the curb perhaps you were saying. *Yes, I, too feel this*
way sometimes. As if all was passing right by me but through a curtain of water.

You could picture her face whoever she was. You could picture yourself
saying the words.

I think about the objects down there, the oceans below us.
The relics of ships—timepieces, bolts of silk decayed past lace, a brass
button with a picture of a lion stamped on it.

The lion of the desert. What is that, you ask? We ask the same
questions in this part of the world.

7.

No. That is what you would have said to me.

8.

You were thinking about work.
You were thinking that perhaps you should take more baths. Get a haircut
so they would not find you so odd.

But they need me, you said. *No one needs anyone,* you said.

9.

You always expected it. That is the other possibility. When you woke
in the night, you could taste the death in your mouth.

It was not like the flavor of blood or dust. It was faintly sweet
like the tooth powder your grandmother used

when you were a boy, disguised with mint, but redolent of decay.

10.

The almond trees, the concrete, the car. These are the only elements
I can reconstruct with any confidence.

Your foot long, second toe attenuated. You lift off. I can assert this
with confidence. You lift off. You are sure you will come down again until
the ball of your foot lifts and—

11.

Congratulations to the first MMM Poetry Contest Winner,
Finalists and Semifinalists! All of these poems may be found at
www.mmminc.org.

Winner:
Renato Rosaldo, "TILT"
(published in print here and online at www.mmminc.org)

The Finalists (anonymously selected by Marcus Cafagña):
Marj Hahne, "Death in Seven Movements"
Marj Hahne, "Face"
Aimee Norton, "In the Name of Cleanliness"
Adam Fieled, "4325 Baltimore Ave."
Mark Thalman, "Encounter"

Semifinalists (anonymously selected by the MMM Poetry Editors):
Trenton Hickman, "We Regret to Inform You"
Nancy Tupper Ling, "Snapshot"
Diane Sahms-Guarnieri, "Another Shirley Temple"
Diane Sahms-Guarnieri, "Rest Stops"
Tamara Oakman, "Casual"

And many thanks to our judge Marcus Cafagña, author of the National Poetry Series winner *The Broken World* (University of Illinois Press, 1996) and *Roman Fever* (Invisible Cities Press, 2001).

TILT

In the hospital room
three TVs screech
their breaking news.

Neon lights gaze
on my sleepless night. One man,
once a jeweler, can't move
his hands. His son grooms him,
snarls about traffic and exits.
The old man's body curls
to a question mark, then,
Help, nurse, help me.
I unfurl into a waltz,
yearn for one more stanza,
but awaken into a heaviness that drags
the floor as I weave
toward the plastic urinal
at the foot of my bed.

I remember trouble
on a walk with Biscuit,
slanting into a slow tilt,
bent in a sideward bow,
how I wobbled
home for a healing sleep.

Caretakers reduce me
to a backless green gown, lift
me onto a gurney, catscan, MRI.
Then, in a basement room, lights glare,
green machines huddle around a monitor.
A white coat inserts

sonar camera, lets it slither down,
says, Swallow hard, assures
me I won't suffocate.

Getting dressed
in shards: I tie shoelaces, button
shirt, lift calf with my hands, aim
foot toward hollow pant leg.

Two days later when my tilt resumes
the doctor says I've had a stroke.
I tell him I'm afraid. He points
the way to Emergency and I walk
without a gyroscope.

Poem

I remember believing I could lose
You in New Orleans
Amid
The bare-breasted coeds, jazz
Funerals, and family fortunes
Built on Tabasco sauce. Today
Fear still
Makes camp
On my gut, I've just got
Fresh culprits to blame.
There are about a thousand
Windows out
Our bathroom window, maybe
More, and I'm a little
Dazed
By the thought of all that
Potential tragedy. And
A man's shout
Up from the street
Covers the clock radio
In the bedroom.

       *   *   *

The President is in town
Tonight, helicopters
Buzz the paralyzed
Traffic, near eye
Level with us
Here on the tenth floor.
My guess
Is that nothing can be seen

Through
The gauzy white curtains
Mo hung
Last month, but
I drop the blinds anyway
Before we put our bodies together.
"Our bodies together,"
That means sex, though
I don't know
What sex means.
Not "my orgasm"
Or "my desire,"
Not "my" anything.
If I wasn't

*   *   *

Here, that might be
Closer. Afterwards
We walk to the kitchen
To wrap the rhubarb pies
Cooling on the stove,
The Christmas lights strewn
Round the window
The only light
Until the refrigerator door
Soaks the brown tile floor in yellow. Now
I'll bet
We can be seen
If anyone cares to look:
She, kneeling there, naked,
Angling the last one
Behind the white wine.

Why I Won't Say I Love You

One boy flips another. In the handclap
of the sensei resides the whole boy and the broken
boy. Trace the grains on the dojo floor: a thought
collapses plight into calliopes. My father

kept his pencils sharp and pointed
to the light. I avoid hospitals and drive
without my glasses. I have a cat
that shuns the easy

ingress. She's smarter than me,
balanced on three legs, one
for sacrifice. I right the fallen
centerpiece: two lilies, a bud cut

for luck, like the boy, who
between breaths, is every possible thing.

Rock Candy

Shadows
play tricks
on unsuspecting snow.

But this light
cannot
be touched

or tugged back
only accumulated
like sugar on string.

Thin
as wild horses
aspens linger,

white socked
icicles
broken at the knee.

On glinted stillness
huffed hover
of their breath.

Stations

Hopper peeled behind it
to scratch its soul
satin sleeved
undereaves

Hovered beneath flimsy depth
as bats looked
back upon
hold the pool of petered light

Know a waiting place
over and over cloned
same species
of starling

And watch its cinched wing
never venture
outside
of stillness

Except to fly off
when we weren't looking
to find what food
makes shadows grow.

Wag

no one mentioned her error
no one ate the overripe fruit

the black page is a famine

the black page is an elegy
the black page is the duke disguised

> > (at this point the play shifts
> > > to prose)

he   is wicked and evil, but likes dogs.

there is no discrimination with dogs,
all sorts — all breeds — all the black, wet
noses in the world please him just the same.

the black page is a dog in heat

this is a troublesome caption

I keep wanting to tell you:
the figure's knot
chose possession
or a tangle

> > in this scenario the figure is
> > the captain & he is unpossessed,

captionless, gentle, almost mute,
— and still has her garments.

the black page is the trunk closed
the black page is his dumb presence
the black page is the doctrine
of the soul sleeping

liminal and latent —
not at all like a body at rest
relinquishing even
the ready-made movement

nothing but possession
without inhabiting the stalk
and shaft of grapheme parts

grafting notes as the creation
of an alms house the black page
is the absence of souls in purgatory

the black page is the wet nose of a dog
and peopling the world with the notion
as though it were as useful as:

a bob of cherries
a bird & a
tennis ball when he is
shabby and out at heels
(in another version: memory fails —

Take-out Fantasy

Your husband finds a piece of newspaper in his mu shu pork and
informs you he wants to take it back. "Let's not spoil our evening,
honey," you say, offering to eat the tainted portion yourself. "After all,
no one ever *died* from eating a little paper," you add, but he is hell-bent
on having his dinner cooked over so you say, "Fine, I'll go!" grabbing
the keys, the half-empty carton, and making sure to slam the door on
your way out, little blue flames of contention sparking at your heels as
you go. In the car you play loud music and blaze through intersections,
your thoughts jumping around inside your head like monkeys on
speed until they settle on the image of a man across town, sitting at a
table in a fancy restaurant, an empty chair facing him with your name
on it, and suddenly you are there in velvet and pearls, the bell of your
hips swinging past islands of pink linen and exploding centerpieces
as you make your fabulous way through the polished crowd to the
man who will save you from it all, only, just as you reach him you
notice he's reading a newspaper and eating egg rolls, the tapered ends
of a pair of chopsticks resting on his lower lip like two thoughtful
fingers that make you think of the man at home, how right now he's
probably reaching down to brush a curtain of hair from the face of
a child drunk with sleep while the dishwasher hums a love-song into
the night, a bowl of unopened fortune cookies waiting for you on the
other side of the door.

Jumping Gun

The government of feeling
casts a decisive unbalanced vote

Kid yourself—dependent
on automatic pilot, but now

choose the warped oars
in the shallow shoals, to drift?

No one can stop your ascent
into your dusty loft   dismember

the wish and feel weak as you
call the terminal at Logan. Stop

your half-assed proposition

as the skiff takes on water

In matters   of love
testify that you do not   think

The Ecology of Mindfulness

How the fingers
form a fist,
the wood chair hits

the upper portion of the wall.
For each minute
that passes the more and less

normal time soothed it becomes,
the spillway opens
on to the canal-

guilt tunnels through
much more than the actual
blow, the wasp of words.

Pyrite & Mica

for my brother

Summers, we camped near gem shows
booked in cheap hotels—blue or black velveted
tables of agate chessboards, malachite in trays,
an onyx menagerie we coveted. By an emptied mine,
crystals sharp as the name our father gave us

to call them: *pyrite*, two confident syllables,
mastery over those winking dice—a fortune
in foundering hope, common name: *fool's gold*.
A pretty fantasy, until a test of hardness
& weight: then, brilliance had to be enough,

true metal untwinned from its image—
what could be enough to satisfy? We wanted
pockets full to rub our fingers on, to hold
all the way home in the new light of the words
we'd learned—*aventurine. Rhodochrosite.*

Reticulated quartz—& facts: *snowflake obsidian*
is volcanic glass. Semi-precious. We scuffed
around the empty, hard, clay lot next door,
unearthing rocks & bursting them,
thinking *iron makes the clay this rusted red.*

There, limestone lay in dull beads: *shell & bone.*
Sometimes, a chunk of quartz, dirt-white like teeth,
or, silvered opaque, a slab of mica, or granite
sequined with it. Fooled—we'd flake its layers,
watch it drift & cling to us like fish-scales,

peel papery, doll-sized windowpanes
to hold to our eyes, grayed monocles.

Poor transparency, call it *isinglass,* or *shelter,*
or *portal,* let its pigment be tint against glare
& dismantle mirages rising on the hot street.

Let it turn solid. *Mineral.* Its sudden beauty,
fraying crumbled edges. We'd gather
what we'd need to build small cities,
twinned, separate: selves we hadn't given
to words. *Mica could double as glass, & shone*

like silver. What didn't fail us? Brilliance lasted
as long as light was a single thing touching down,
was rough & silvered in our hands,
let them make what they could, let them grow
strange to each other as each cell'd repeat itself,

double helices doubling & wrenched apart,
the membranes translucent, permeable, distinct,
defining. What we are now, we were then.
Replication. Division. We rescue each other,
eye-dimmed spectators, builders of forms.

The saw that cut rock would not cut skin.
It was never lost, that name we couldn't say,
that dark shape that rose in the paler dark
of our eyes in sleep. *Solder & flux.* In time,
even trees would turn to stone. What we trusted.

A Gap in Being

When he comes home
from the trenches, this falling
hostage of myths, nearly erect,
bloodied, thrown,
a pursuer of wisdom once,
kindler of scientific futures,
this heroic pose
oozing now
no longer dances
in divine wonder.

His wars
on his kindred
splinter vision,
mutilate torsos,
ape
his wars on the shrinking earth
leave him with a skull
fabricated
without a trace
of the lived sacred.

Is his a passage
in eclipse,
his island
a native of nothing;
his genocidal schemes
do they make him
a master of oblivion.

P'uhonua, Kona Coast, Hawai'i

A place of refuge, a second chance,
where no blood may be shed, a space
sacred before King Kamehameha
where royalty possessed that spiritual power called mana.

If you outwait folly you might just live,
understand how often a sacred burial
ground is beneath so many steps.

Imagine this planet as a gate of refuge
from total war, a second chance, where
no blood anymore may be shed,
where non-violence toward all living
beings is the law of our breathing.

Might we all then be priests
absolving each other for our
daily injustices, our blinding inhumanities?

Nostalgia

Of course we are beautiful in our remembering
—how my hair fell across your chest, how the sky
was tinged with pink. Sometimes I believe
we rose out of our bodies then, but I am wrong.
These are my loved mountains giving in to streams,
to rivers, to the inevitable ocean. I cling
to the pictures I carry of them—the land's
slope and give, the way pines also cling
to curve and inclination and somehow I am back
at desire. I cannot say enough what ease
the night air gave us, how fog caught
in the valleys, at the lips. But the fierce shape
of memory changes each time we play
the movies our skin made on the bright screen
behind our eyes. Better these mountains now,
fields with black flies and crickets.

By Dust

I would get down on all fours and crawl headfirst
into lint traps that were mine to empty,
each steam-driven cubbyhole swirling
with particle dust. I who cut class
to work at the campus Laundromat
for the freshman I'd once held in contempt.
In a kind of coffin I would lay,
without shame, out of breath, on my back
beneath king-size dryers, overheating.
And the students staying there at the dorm
would shoot me passing glances since it's rude
to stare at a man with gray skin, at a face
masked by a bandanna and by dust.
No stranger to their disco lifestyle, I craned
my neck inside one trap after another
in case a few coins had trickled down
from designer pockets like a bad tip.
I never begrudged them their ivy halls
so long as I didn't end up someone's servant
the way mi abuela had when she first came
to this country. A Spanish speaker in an age
of flappers, she waited on the blue bloods
using the ladies room. By suffering
their pride and prejudice, she sheltered me.
Were she still alive, I'd like to think
my Anna Corona would forgive
the college kid who dropped out of school
now that I am el professor, now that the sleeves
of my shirt are smudged with nothing but chalk,
the dust of a knowledge I'd rather forget.

La Cucaracha

When I recall my baby sister
singing it I don't think of the cockroach,
antennae and six legs on the run
each time we tiptoed the blind
bowling alley of a hallway
and switched on the light.

What I picture is an old car
run out of gas on the desert,
and inside it the mestizo men
who took up arms against all landlords
then disappeared into the Mexican hills,
that ditty of the revolution.

Cézanne's Skulls

How beautiful it is to paint a skull!
—P. Cézanne

Not memento mori
But pure form: eye sockets
Are pockets of wind
Stars sift through.
This is still
Life: no lemon peels
In sight, no slabs of meat
On an orange table.
Skulls: a pyramid,
Off-white, off-black
At night.

Epiphany 2002

In the caves of Tora Bora
Afghan soldiers sit
Backs to the damp wall
Legs across the blue
Trees of life that multiply
On kilims tossed like jewels
Across the stone floor.
A goat is tethered
To a gun. Meanwhile
In Boston the sky
Has gone from fish skin
To striations of clam:
A storm hangs at the edge
But hasn't arrived.

Pot-house Logic

All those dry months,
newly unshakeable, contemplative on
a flea-speckled bed, cuddling the cats.
Fly, flew unafraid, fingernails became
normal; anxiety, physiologically
impossible. Lists and
less manic plans, lawn mowing with
some regularity. There was no talk of
the opposite sex. There was no talk of
sex, period. How dead
was the patient, though, down there?

What a horrible relief it is to find her again at
the party, sans bra. Sure enough, the
recycling is piling up again, all
red and gold aluminum. Drink up,
and whirl away, in a trail of American Spirit and
muffled burp. Go to a new land, and set up the
same old teepee.

Does (or doesn't) each buried secret
make life more mysterious?

Of the Many Ways Back to the Body

Like reappearing faces in a deck of cards
or those things about your face
you can't help,
you were looking
for the model smile, you got systemic beauty.

Those remaining trails of ice you find
in unsprung parts of the forest.

The patio is our newest
archetype. Through deck slats, I see
the top of your head,
spiral made by your hair there.
Your sweet cowlick.

Low pressure and its shy pockets
of cooler air.

All the trees don their halos
and lingerie, unable to trace
their last partners. Sex drops
into its navy-colored cavern.
We're grateful for the humidity.

Anything to do with flooding.

The day's center, lavender
and opulent with weather,
so preparatory.
Cloud categories overwhelm me.
Your hands willowy.

The rivering of noises
always outside of us.

This is the rush
of wind and temporary
identification. Engendering
your ear, as you breathe
so carefully to preserve a posture.

The Bluffs

All day
we wander the bluffs,

standing above the birds,
cutting their circles
in the air below us.

Together, with the birds,
we watch the earthbound creatures
scurrying from place to place,

passing each other
on the interstate,
rushing their lives along.

Then we lean back
into the hands
of fronds and grass,

practice belonging
to the sky.

Exhaustion

If she could use
her hands to fasten
a button twist a knob
scribble a letter
to tell me she dreams

about tailpipes
thirteen parts assembled
again and over
like a broken dance
of two palms

stroking rubbery backs
fingers bowing
to partners swollen
with gnarled collapse
snapping delicate cylinders

joints in place
for the socket and bend of it
as she dismantles her own
one occupation at a time

even before they tell her
with owning fists
to speed the quota
because flesh is thick
in a town that has no fire

just cold furnaces
and breadsinners
with lottery eyes or
bingo on their breath

so where can she go
if the work of her hands
is meant for reaching
the liquid grasp
of all things falling

Litany

Agatha of scissors and shorn breasts
Brigid of dairymaids, Blaise of wool
Cecilia, song from your severed head
Dymphna of lunatics, Dennis of frenzy
Egwin, of Ethelred, patron of keys
Fiacra of florists
Gall of cocks
Hilary of backward and snake-bitten children
Iwi of immoveable relics
Januarius of blood banks
Kentigern, a.k.a. Mungo, patron of rings and salmon
Luke of butchers
Margaret of breach births
Nynia, whose sole hands erected Candida Casa
Odilia, Ottillia, Odo the Good, Odilo, Olaf the Fat
Pancras of pancreas
Quenton of ills, of drills, of quills
Rita of desperation
Sebastian invoked against plague, in the plague
months
Thomas of cantaloupe
Ursula, anorexia
Valentine, wasps, Vitus, asps
Wilfred of national bickering
Xavier, queerly of torches and water
Yenaya of parrots, sugar cane, lox
Zita, bare-handed, the fiery ovens

Morning Sutra

She is dreaming me
into my uncle
while I read
the violet sutra,
sponging her forehead
with a hot cloth.
He presses her
petal dress,
soaps the gold
from her finger,
pulls the needle
from her frayed vein
as her face slackens
into the quiet lid
of a closed box.
But he left this room
long ago,
so I pretend
to be him for her
finding the roundness
of her face,
knowing her breath
will come.

The Nun

Some dead glide by
Somnambulating through the gaps
Between events.

Here the nun's habit promises
A hereafter of profound-toned bells
Ringing out until they wave the whole air.

The memory behind the habit
Twists the treads.

The dark stair
In the sanctuary leads nowhere.

She climbs
Catching the dead near the edges
Of her prayers, near the fringes
Of habit, near the dark cough of the bells.

Her habit is a cloak
Woven in the threads of heaven
Where meaning skuts down the street.
Like leaves.

Her cloak enfolds and enfolds
Threads upon threads; her love,
Unwrapped, moves out toward those who
Touch the stones of the abbey in bliss.

Sweet, this healer, to other realms leaves,
And her hands are graceful and small.
The healed return to the broken sky;
The waves, nearing the hill, cease.

Midwinter

I feel my body cooling. The sun has turned away.

Weaning my daughter, I held her in my arms, refused her
my breast. Now she smashes a glass in the road and drives off.

My father's packing, leaving home, selling the house not for sale,
getting out of bed to dress at midnight.

                          In the lake below
deep booms of ice cracking, lightning with nowhere to go.

I used to twirl the long handle of the vise on his workbench,
watch the two halves approach, ridged faces lock in the middle.

I cannot breathe, cannot reach to touch their backs. Too delicate, this
act of leaving.

                  I feed goats in the morning, knead bread, bank the
fire at night. Someone has to stay.

For a Song

I'm a piano wire plucked by winds
inside my father's head. Rehersing late into night.
My daughter thrashes inside her sleep, sweet canary
in the mineshaft. Zen monks wrote haiku
in the moments before death. Oh, for a dream.
This reality's relentless. I'd give it up for a song.
From the cellar come strains of the last aria:
the lovers, sealed in the tomb, are singing.

What is Mine

a constellation of hooves,
wet arrhythmic breath
against my neck, membranes
thorned with raw silk mountain air,
the ripple of pine, fissures
of bristling light—a messenger,
a pressure inside—the slope
of shoulders, back and haunch,
the gentle tooth-filled maw
of a beast whose shuttered gaze
is a turnstile, the soft layers of an aperture.

Mambo #5 in Berlin

Drugged fabulist: hallucinations
of two railroad cars coupling, three jolts
drunk on a quaff of thunder, on rapid fire
confabulations, speaker cones near blow-out.
As the band below the stone shell
of the Gedaechtniskirche tower
hits hullabaloo, understatement vanishes
and everyone's heart skips a beat.
Double or nothing, no Latin rhythm, this!
Otto Dix rises from the dead,
George Grosz wanders by in drag,
Klee strips, Kandinsky does his mambo.
Time takes off—no telling where or when.
Black American, mic in hand, has the crowd
in a lock no '30s tyrant could spring.
He calls the tune. In step, everyone mouths the words:
three Chinese teens, Ghanaians with nothing to sell,
a Turkish woman almost out of her *higab,*
German girls on the brink of orgasm,
beer stand staff twisting like reeds in a wind,
two Indians doing the Shiva.

As the Gedaechtniskirche strikes ten,
heads bop like clappers against
an invisible bell: fat man on a roll, fatima,
fabian, gypsies, Russians out from under.
Three bums crash the party of their life,
police van wraps its siren around the crowd.
Now there's no way out or letting go;
bass, drums, singer and keyboard in control,
the crowd in their thrall, joyous slaves
mob the music, the throbbing trance.
How easy it is, how perilous
in the wrong hands as in 1933.

Sister

what I want you to understand is this—
the cellar was colder than you may think,

empty taste of earth pulled oxygen out
till my lungs were flat, fit in small spaces.

what I want you to know is the corners
quivered with dark growth, spiders and beetles

huddled over pale, yellowed sacs. There were
bushels of potatoes, spindled shoots stretched.

standing above me, hand on the light switch,
you laughed. you must not have known that the dark

would stay twenty years, a hand cold and wet
always pressed on some piece of my flesh.

Ghazal about Tails

Teeny me. I was once in Eden, enslaved by the smell of Eve in the morning.
She never heard the ballads I planned to whisper in her ear. Instead, my tail

was caught under Adam's foot. How could it be that God
      gave me such a brain
in this body? I have the heart of Caesar. The eternity in my skin
      like an elephant. The tail,

of course, of a mouse. I am partially lucky in the year of the rat.
I've thought about writing a personal ad: Sweet voice. Great at telling
      tall tales.

Call me. I will be your slippery, gray baby. Once, I was mistaken
      for a potato.
A wife grabbed me for her soup-kettle, then shrieked when her hand
      touched my tail!

I am your Romeo. I am an Adonis closeted in a rodent's frame.
      Cheese, cheese.
I dream of escaping from my life through a hole and on the other side
      I am huge, my tail

thunders on the ground, punctures the hearts of my enemies.
      Unlike you, I know my mother loved me
because she didn't eat me. I can smell every creature on earth.
      Here's a tale:

Mouse from the Latin, *Mus, musculus* meaning sack, meaning testicle,
      meaning flavor of sex.
The best part of this tale: It's always been me from the start.

What Remains

This morning a shallow breath came to me like a wave
of light, one shadow of its former self, far off.
That was me complete.
                              Release. It is no more
than a fingerprint, a moment's grasp, a hand slapping waves,
                                        a small shadow drifting
through the light of a deeper shadow. It is one stitch
among the mist, it contemplates sunset.

Shadows release, the first idea of light.
Hieroglyphs of night condense into horsetail points and bury their heads in
              like ticks,
packets of beginning along the rocky ends and weaves of shore. Scoters whistle

beyond the waves all morning; to pull an ethereal thread through their pierce
                                        is my humble beginning.

This morning a shallow breath came to me like a wave,
rose to mingle with the eternal functionaries
and flowers; with Joyce and Beckett offering mild suggestions
to the circuitous conversations and breezes; among the lighter ideas of air
some of the finer points of rainfall get worked out
over that far deep, the Irish Sea.
                              Two crows loom
on the oak's wide branch, inky points and bloom-ends,
bury their beaks in wide space. Nothing glistens like they do.
Above the delicate nibs of their nostrils
steam riches, and above that clouds
                              white as paper dissipate into sun.

I move among their feathers and nestle in, eyes-first. Complete for once
I see myself through the window. Carrying on and nervous
I disappear.

Imagine Rome just now, among marshy fog and time.
The coliseum grows meaningless, fading, along with everything else,
into the slow beat of a vendor's cough.

> At once you know it all, and the
> boyhood memory of ocean,

the breaker from behind, the crumpling light

> airless and alien silence of yourself

becomes a reassurance;

> the curling becomes a line,

and unfolding within it you again touch childhood
with one bare hand, smell in yourself the sea

> as your fingertips linger, buds

on a winesap slip.

The speed which is a thought beyond

> slowness, a slowness beyond

patience, beyond camel or snail or baobab, beyond fruit-bat or parchment-curl;
the unending patience of plankton
which is the sure gulping slowness of stars.

This morning a shallow breath came to me like a wave
lopped ashore, whorl and steam of the endless;

> apple-buds break open,

purl and foam

> of another April sky.

A tide-bore runs my memory and settles for a moment frothing, the chin of
      every orchid
in attendance over the fluid curves and each series of fluid curves,
and the reservations where no air curves any longer, and the past spaces
of body which are no longer, curled inward beyond all memory, even that of
      flowers
which is that of chrysalis-motion and the singular perception of caterpillars
      dying quietly
                into themselves.

Release. It is no more.
The fingers of a broad hand withdraw, and I hold you shaking.

An accumulation of cumulus spots our memory.
In green relief against the sky, the sharp points of horsetails agree with you,
      then me,
a teeming of fingers unclenched, pointing out nothing,
                        return beyond themselves.
I will also one day teem, also return beyond myself.
Understand, I intone through the pressure of joint-thought:
all at once is not, in the end, enough.
I will fail and come to
myself, I will be empty as stone, solid as sky.
Lost patterns of breath, my fingerprints-in-waiting, will carry me off.

Miles away the sea spits back into rhythm.
My breath loses me, and melts into spring.

There is much to escape from, seeing how every shadow
is a thing's compressed history nightly gathered into itself

and daily cast over the world like a net,

                                 floating with the current

yet catching nothing for any length of time; never the current, never itself.

I am my breath's shadow

                    and here is mine, balled in my palm, a caged fog

illuminated from within,

               as if by persistence.

I expect nothing of it, and am satisfied, and let it go.

Every breath undoes me and I increase. Last year's oak leaves drop

as new buds bunch beneath them. A rising fog

will persist all season over the warm sound, muffling insignificance.

The silence of one bell clapping leaves me

shirtless in the warmth, pulls me out rearranged. I am a scent

caught in the April air, both lilac and bell-lily, and the silence, touched,

                                 swoons in the wings.

The gentle soliloquy of April is nearly over

and I am nearly born. The pear-buds break open

like dropped china, a breath

of nowhere filled with sun-scent again, again released from the tide-winds of

        winter.

This morning a shallow breath came to me like a wave

and settled in like petal-strokes of light,

propped on lapsed shadows. A tide of shadows relieves me,

I will think no more; there is a world rising and with it I rise.

The scoter's wings release all weight, and fold

                          headfirst into Puget Sound.

Unsuitable Biography, Written in the Latter Part of the 20th Century

Show me a Polaroid of your suffering: a burnt child, a limping dog,
a departure at night, two suitcases, a blue coat. The latter a last
possession of your golden age. Elsewhere, people say, it's worse.
But even this is enough.

A taxi pulls away from the curb. It doesn't matter who's inside.
I forgot to tell you this: nothing matters. Nothing, except skin,
voice, glance. That's not quite true, of course, and I don't believe
it myself but it's August, and behind the saturated green wheat fields

lies a tempting horizon which allows us to rise above the gloomiest
of weather forecasts or biblical floods or snow in Miami and all
end-time predictions, and be happy. Just be happy, for God's sake!
It's never so bad it can't get worse.

No Fear, the shirt says. But then this courage bleeds in the wash
and a horoscope is consulted: Trust your emotions. A romantic
interlude brightens your afternoon. Tacitus tells us about runed
sticks, thrown and read like the migration of birds.

Amphitheaters collapse, and, earlier, the Tower of Babel. In 1902,
Mount Pelee erupts, flattening Martinique's capitol city and killing
all residents, except the city's only prisoner. In that year,
the silk tail, a flashy bird at home in extreme northern latitudes

appeared in mass quantities, fleeing south to escape the arctic winter.
(The history of doom can be written in a language of feathers.)
Three days after the eruption, Jacques, the prisoner, speaks to birds,
confesses the theft, the rape, the murder.

100% Negro

are the T-shirts the blue-eyed
brown people wear. The secrets
in the sugar cane fields sucked
into white roots. In the sun
we dance without shirts   only white
pants   throwing our legs in circles barely
missing necks   faces   arms. Those who watch
sing   pluck the *berimbau* and thump drums   rattle hollow
gourds. Not too long ago we sharpened
machetes on rocks   crimson lines keeping us alive.

How our art was banned. Those other
blue eyes so wary   fearful. It is the
forest   by ourselves where we re-remember
Angola   parrots flying above us.

The Headless Saints

Agave water crests
beneath azure. Black moths

return to hills   islands waiting
to lose their vapor coronets   snow

pines. I will spool each cloud
into thread   cloth   clothes.

We will walk quietly through
town   bare soles. There is so much

to search for   paradise
in poverty's hot house.

Chop indigo   smear the juice
on cement walls   tree trunks.

Remember seas   the salt
that preserved those bodies

washing to shore. They are headless
but have learned to walk   climb

coconut palms   a green sweet harvest.
How holy they are naked   born

in a garden without unnecessary knowledge.
In a church they gather. We watch

with hands covered in the stickiest blue
(no fallen sky). A Pope has not

made us saints   we neither want
nor need one to do so but here in

this town of stars   the smooth
feet of our dead against this

burned ground   there is
enough light here.

Raison d'Être

after Collins

This is the start. Almost anything can happen.
On stage, the house lights dim and a curtain rises.
The first tomato of the year. A boom of thunder.
This is where you realize you are falling in love.
This is January, the green digital clock beeping
you into Monday at 6:00 a.m., 6:00 a.m., 6:00 a.m.
This is the first time you saw her and the last time
you saw her. This is first guitar chord of the opening
song on the first date of a month long tour.
The cool sand on a clean beach. This is where
you learn how to ask questions
in order to get what you want.

This is the middle. The stomach moaning for lunch,
a child with bloody elbows, a thrown stone beginning
its descent. This is the turning point of the film
where you think, *this is starting to get good.*
This is the gas station bathroom on a five hour drive.
This is the bridge, the refrain, the leap from a perfectly
good plane. This is the batch of tomatoes that becomes
a gift for a friend. Here is a time to think, *my God
what have I done?* Make your substitutions.
Get the right players on the field.
This is the apology, suspended
in midair like a cloud.

And this, this is the end. This is the guitarist
smashing the amp, the last lip of the sun over the hills.
Here we discover our reason for being, the black mascara
on a widow's cheek, and the solemn bow to the crowd.

Here is the moon, December, midnight. This is Friday,
the exhale after too long a wait. This is the coda,
the swan howling at the lake, a moon bloated
with deathbed prayers. This is like a beginning.
A circle of sorts. Here is where you realize love
assumes the shapes of flowers in damp backyards,
denying the temptation to wilt.

Three Dreams of Korea:
Notes on Adoption

1.
This one happens in morning
as a crow nearby wakes me,
calling *God, God,*
look at this:
I am on the steps of a church,
wrapped in Monday's *Korea Times*
telling of the drought in Pusan.
You can live by the water
and still die of thirst, and I,
there on the cold brick steps,
am dying. But dying
means the presence of breath.
This one happens on a day
of independence, Hangul Day
in Seoul, where girls in purple
satin hanboks parade through
downtown streets, and in this
dream, I make eye contact with
every single one of them.
I am on the steps for an hour
in this dream. Another boy,
five years older than I, rides
a bicycle in the parade, trailing
trailing the girls.
He sees me.
He winks,
as if he knows how
everything will end.

2.

This one happens in the evening
just as daylight surrenders to the moon,
and the flute of dusk arrives.
It is cool.
I am wrapped in a sky blue blanket,
so whoever finds me thinks kindly
of whoever left me.
The one who finds me is a nun.
She opens the door, looking
beyond me
into the tired night,
then looks down.
She gasps softly.
She says, *ahneyong,* you sweet
beautiful child. She bends
down like an angel
and takes me
into her arms.

3.

This one happens in the cruelest moment
of the day, as heat curls flowers
into dirt. A man, drunk
with despair, screams at the sun.
His sorrow is a collage of
moths and ants, crawling
from his face to his chest.
I watch from the steps.
It is the year of the dog
and I am a part of it:
unable to speak
but an expert at listening
to the old man from Laos who sits
on the steps two buildings down:

he is telling another man
how Hmong children become human
in the third day of life,
after the soul calling ceremony
and the burning of animal flesh.
He smokes from a pipe
and closes his eyes as he inhales.
I can hear all of this.
I can hear a woman rustling inside the church.
She is a dancer, so she speaks with her hands.
I hear her rise, sweetly
from her knees to her feet.
This means she believes
in dreams. I hear her
slide her hand, sweetly
along her hair. This means
she believes in the sun.
I hear her move towards me
and place her open palm on the door.
This means she welcomes me.
This means she believes
in the miracle of possibility.

Hunger Strike

"Every mandarin that drops, I pick it up and hold it,
and hope that my daughter will come home to eat it."
                    —Mehmet Semer, Turkey

The body more like a piano
                    you used
to carry for the world
                    to play (infinite
symphony) set
          down now.

     Voices, fading   headlines,
weak tea, daddy's plaintive pitch,
          a window   view of the sea:

          every ghost   strikes
its chord.   What breaks you
          waits to be   broken,

a tangled nest of wire   dried
to dust   like the coastal reeds
          of Marmara.

You once loved   to swim
the ocean harmonies;

even memory turns
                    to touch—
the pain,   the float away
          and return,   the pain.

Coda. Echo fade   into air.
You can do   nothing—the world

more
like a body   you used
       to carry.
Wait for   liberation, day
when bergamot breezes
       shiver the keys

and no longer sound
you. A polished   wooden shell.

The Day Allen Died

I was in London looking for a lost home & the paper said
you had inoperable liver cancer & it was 4 months to a year
& that was a real shock I didn't even know you were sick
or that you were such a deep part of my world I didn't know
I went over to Bunhill Fields & stood in front of Blake's tomb
& told him about it you would have gotten off on
the Hieronymousness of the scene all the old old gravestones
companionably crowded up against each other
right smack in the middle of the howling Moloch madness of the City
like an island of sanity peaceful with the Buddha's peace
at the foot of this great black death robot slab of flats under construction
the wind whipping its plastic wrapping into snapping & flailing
frantically like an announcement of some disaster
& later in my little pub I read you had died that day
I didn't know then that I was with 2 dead poets
I couldn't have known & maybe anyway it wasn't yet so
London's 5 hours earlier than Manhattan I don't know
maybe you were still alive then on your last day
still better than a good poet a good man
when the caretaker said I'm locking the gates now mate

A Dog's Life

November, 1957. It's cold, flesh-cracking cold. The barren steppes roll off into the icy haze, unmarked, save for a few low clumps of dead grass and three or four brick buildings. Light like flint, clutters the plain and a polar wind slams at the bricks over and over. Nothing changes. It seems, nothing here ever changes. As if in argument, the center of this land of sleet and ice begins to burn deep orange. Miles off, the light gathers itself and roasts the thin air. Kerosene and liquid oxygen come together as though they have been waiting for this moment for a million years. A gray hare raises its nose to the wind, turns to see the light.

At the flame and the noise, men inside one of the small blockhouses run to windows filled with smoked glass. As they watch, the fire burns stronger and brighter. Seconds pass—nothing more happens. Though no word has been spoken, each of the men inside is afraid that nothing more will happen. Finally—a millimeter at a time—the fire begins to rise. Slowly, so slowly it seems certain to fail, the flame pushes itself and a two-stage rocket from the frozen ground at Baikonur Cosmodrome, USSR. The hare lowers its ears and its eyes fill up with flame.

Behind the blistered bricks, the men turn to one another and smile. Overhead, the light grows dimmer, and dimmer, then disappears altogether. Sputnik 2 has left this world. Two stages, ten tons of metal, 253 tons of kerosene and liquid oxygen, 1,118 pounds of aluminum nose cone, and twelve-pounds of living flesh.

November, 2000. It is a mild dry day. Just beyond Pueblo, Colorado, my wife and I are headed south, toward New Mexico for Thanksgiving. The light has gathered over the mountains to the west. A cool wind is blowing down their shoulders and everything smells of sage and an early winter. Colorado slides quickly past our windows. We speak of times past and times to come. As we talk, I am scanning a road map, hoping to pinpoint our whereabouts. An odd and nearly useless habit of mine.

Suddenly, something appears in the road before us. Gina swerves to the left to avoid it. I look up from the map I've been studying and see that we've driven partway into the median, at about 75 miles per hour. Weeds are whipping past slapping the front, then bottom, of the car. Gina swerves back onto the roadway. The car twitches oddly to the left, and we are abruptly in the right lane of the southbound highway. Gina reaches again for control of the 4,000 pounds of steel and vinyl beneath us. She tries hard to bring the car back in line with the road. Again it twitches. Again she reaches.

Time itself splits open.

I have no past. There is only future.

Slowly, the car heels over onto its side—Gina's side. Sound returns like a fist. The windows shatter. Every piece we'd packed for the trip is in motion inside the car. Gathering speed, the car quickly flips three, four times. The world around us loops past our windows. Only we are fixed, all else is motion. Again the silence. A computer hovers behind me, in free fall. A pen is rotating just past my fingertips in the center of nothing. Gina and I still, pinned to the instant by the nylon straps of our seat belts.

Suddenly, the spinning stops. Gravity slaps a final time at us and our Explorer comes to rest upside down in the dirt in the median. The wheels spin, the car sighs, yellow dust pours in through the shattered windows. All that was with us is strewn across a hundred yards of short-grass prairie. Everything is red or yellow or black. I reach to my side and fumble with the seat belt and finally release it. I drop back into time and land on my head in the now foreshortened cab of the Explorer. I reach through the broken window and pull myself out into the oddly warm dirt, the strangely yellow and green grass. I do not know if my wife is dead, alive, in this state, on this planet. It is quiet again.

I saw Gina in Pueblo twice after that. The first time we accidentally passed in the hall, each of us strapped to a white-sheeted gurney. Each of us pushed by green-clad people with severe expressions hanging like bats from their faces. We held hands for a moment. We squeezed each other's hands, and then we were wheeled off in different directions. The last time I saw her there, she was paralyzed by medication and stuffed full of plastic tubes. She couldn't speak or move. I squeezed her hand. She stared at the tiled ceiling and the empty face of the fluorescent tubes. Then she was gone in a clatter of helicopter blades and rush of cold air.

"Will she die?" I asked as they wheeled me back into the rings of the CT scanner.

"She might," the doctor responded. "But if she survives the first forty-eight hours, she may make it. Her bruised lungs are her greatest enemy just now," he said solemnly. He was wrong.

Forty-eight hours later, I catch up with Gina in Denver. Pieces of her are missing. Gina—her right hand strapped to her bed, a thick vinyl tube pushing air into her lungs, her legs swaddled like two swollen baby Jesuses, and her left arm taped and strapped tightly against her chest—looks to me like God himself has beaten her, repeatedly. Her face is a topograph of bruises. A piece of her intestine is gone and her belly is split like a burst purple grape. I can see inside of my wife.

Gina's bed crouches among a cluster of such beds, arranged like the petals on a daisy—black-and-blue, with plastic hoses stuck in each petal. Over each body a bank of lights burns surgically. Skin-colored tile stretches over the concrete beneath and dribbles off toward the waiting room. Darkness seeps from the walls. Everything happens slowly. People, in pale green, move from place to place, following some choreography I can't fathom. Nothing changes.

Soiled dressings, spilt urine, clotted blood. Isopropyl alcohol. The smells of Hell.

For the first time, I seriously consider the possibility that we didn't survive at all. The reality that this might be our punishment.

I sit. The people around me change faces, but they keep telling the same stories. I understand that the stories are terribly important. In spite of my stupor, I understand that, and I try to listen. But the stories are too complicated.

The first two days in ICU, Gina imagined herself blind. The darkness was that complete. In reality, the pounding she received bruised her face so badly that both eyes were swollen tightly shut. The whispers, the people in transit, the noise, the smell. Heironymus Bosch. The only lights that flickered were those behind her eyes, flickered over a landscape no one else has seen.

I was the first to tell Gina about her eyes.

Instead of giving her back her sight, the huddled doctors divided her up with the knives of their whispers and argued among themselves about who got the first shot at her. There was a "back guy," a "shoulder guy," a "knee guy," and a "lung guy." The "lung guy" more or less had his way for the first two days after Gina arrived. The bruises and the pneumothoraxes demanded that.

Today, the "back guy" wants a crack at my wife.

Five of Gina's vertebrae fractured when our car flipped. The "back guy" worries that if her back isn't fixed as quickly as possible, the broken bones might damage Gina's spinal cord. If that happens, she might be paralyzed for real. Probably he's right. I have no way of knowing. The night all of this happens, I am in Fort Collins—trying to shake some of the foggy-headedness and the hallucinations that are chasing me. The doctor calls to ask if it is okay with me if he splits Gina's back. From his tone, it is obvious to me that he thinks I should be there, in Denver—not Gina's sister. While trying to make sense of what he's asked, I am watching a broad-leaf plant turn into a large, black dog with slobbering lips and curled pink tongue. Eyes like roasted chestnuts. I tell the doctor to go ahead.

He hangs up. I lay back and wait for the drugs to take effect.

That night, the "back guy" cracks the skin above Gina's spine, lays in two metal plates, and drives ten stainless steel screws, big around as pencils, into her spine with a power drill. Then he opens up her hip, carves pieces of some bone there, and packs the bone chips between her bolted vertebrae. Gina's hip will hurt worse than her back for a long time to come.

When I meet the "back guy" in Gina's room a couple of days later, he tells me he wants to show me a picture of my wife. Apparently, he has forgiven me for my absence, or, more likely, forgotten. He sticks a black chunk of film into the clips of a light box. The picture shows nothing but my wife's lower spine and the steel he has added to her busted bones. He seems very proud of the steel. He seems very pleased with his photo of my wife.

We hold hands when we can. But we never speak to one another. We can't speak to one another, because of the ventilator tube pushing Gina's lungs open and closed. The tube blocks her larynx. She can say nothing. Most of the time, there are only the two of us and the wheeze of the machine breathing life into her, then sucking it back out of her. One morning, Gina slides a piece of paper into my hand.

"I need to get out of here. They're trying to kill me," is scribbled across the blue paper.

How can I argue with her?

The engineers gave Laika air enough to last for six or seven days. Sputnik 2 would likely orbit Earth for six or seven months. On Earth, time was short. In space time would be no factor. The Americans had made fun of the Russians' first satellite—it weighed little and held only two tiny transmitters. The U.S. assured the Russians that U.S. scientists weren't wasting their time on anything so trivial. That made everyone in Russia angry. But it made the Soviet Premier especially angry. Nikita Kruschev himself insisted on a new satellite—larger and with something alive on board—to be launched within one month.

They would show the Americans.

Orders were orders. People began throwing things together. A launch vehicle was assembled from an existing R-7 ICBM—once targeted, perhaps, at the U.S.A. A payload capsule was welded together. A Tral-D telemetry system was bolted in to transmit data back to the Earth during 15 minutes of each orbit. Two spectrophotometers were added to measure solar radiation (both ultraviolet and X-ray) and cosmic rays. And finally a television camera was mounted in the "passenger" compartment. The camera would transmit 100-line video frames at 10 frames per second. Then it was time to find a passenger.

Two men were sent to Moscow. At a local shop, they bought a

kilo of meat and walked back onto the city's streets. In a nearby alley, they enticed a dog—part terrier, part Samoyed, all cur—into their van. There they fed her the rest of the meat and chained her to the van for the trip back to Baikonur.

Now that they knew the size of the animal they would hurl into space, the men began to fashion a harness for the dog. When that was done, they modified the passenger compartment to fit the mutt, added a generator to provide oxygen for a few days, and a plastic bottle that would hold some water. An air cooler was welded in and then a food container, not very large. Recovery of the satellite and the dog was never even considered. Not nearly enough time to plan something so complex. There was time only for blasting the dog and her machine into space and into the faces of the Americans. As though she knew, the dog barked constantly. So, the men at Baikonur named her Laika—Russian for "barker."

Pictures were taken so all the world might know. Laika lay, looking almost happy, inside her capsule. The harness wasn't in place, of course, and the lid of the capsule was off. They gave her lots of food for the pictures. But not at other times. Her weight was still of utmost importance.

The ascent from Baikonur Cosmodrome is more than Laika thinks she can stand. She is crushed to the floor, her ears pinned to her head, her jaw slammed shut by the flat slap of gravity. Fear like she has never known floods her mind as the ship inches toward the heavens. Saliva runs between her lips, through her teeth, onto the floor of the capsule.

Inside the twelve-foot high by six-foot wide cone Laika understands none of what is happening. Or why the men in Moscow grabbed her while she tried to eat what they seemed to offer so freely, then swept her off to Baikonur and packed her into this capsule. At the moment, though, the roar and the ragged rattling of steel against steel have stripped her of all curiosity. She has space only for now.

The "shoulder guy" got the next shot at Gina.

From the very first, the man who did the work did not believe Gina's shoulder could be fixed. He told me that before the surgery even began. In the waiting room, at the top of the stairs. Beneath us, a hundred people sat in poorly padded chairs waiting for a turn to speak with a nurse or visit with a doctor. A hundred people afraid of their own bodies. A hundred people with no one else to turn to. A hundred people from every nook and cranny in Denver. And above them all, we spoke of the fate of a single woman's shoulder and it meant everything.

"I'll try to repair her shoulder," he said matter of factly, "but I may have to replace it. If that happens, then I don't know. I'm less enthusiastic about that outcome."

"Why?" I asked.

"Prostheses just don't work very well in people your wife's of age. No one really understands it. She's too young for this surgery."

"Oh."

But something had to be done. Time was running out.

I sat back down with my sister, her husband, and my sister-in-law. I tried to tell them what the surgeon had told me. None of us understood. Among the soiled fabrics in the waiting room, we sat with others equally confused and waited.

The surgeon reminded me of his pessimism again immediately after the surgery. We met this time in the surgery waiting area—a mildly purple-and-gray space where eight or ten of us sat with bowed heads while people we barely knew worked our loved ones over with knives. The lights hummed overhead. People came and went. Men and women in green scrubs would arrive periodically like large caterpillars and speak softly to one group or another in the waiting room. The people who heard either cried or smiled. Then, usually, they left, holding one another's hands.

Gina's surgeon, short, dark-haired, in his green scrubs, Italian, looked at me through eyes brown as my mother's and told me to give up.

"I tried," he says, "to save her shoulder. But there just wasn't enough good bone left to hold the screws. Her bones are really not very good."

Her fault. She should have seen it coming, done more.

"So we replaced her shoulder." With what? I wanted to ask, but didn't.

"But, like I told you, I'm not very optimistic about how that will turn out. Not at all. She's too young. These things don't go very well in people like your wife."

"What does that mean, actually?" I asked.

"I don't expect she will regain much use of her shoulder."

And he showed me, lifting his limp-wristed hand to elbow level, his upper arm tight against his body.

"Something about like that is average."

"How is she?"

"She's doing just fine."

"What does that mean?" I wanted to ask, but, again, I didn't. I was afraid this time he might show me.

Instead, I made up my mind that he was wrong. Averages made no difference. Gina wasn't ever average. Making up my mind, though, made no difference—to him, to Gina, to what was once her shoulder.

As he walked away, I couldn't shake the image of Gina's shoulder lying in a stainless-steel garbage can somewhere.

He could have been wrong, though, that doctor. He could have been.

As it reaches for the blackness above this Earth, Laika's ship groans and cracks like a breaking wrist. The brutal forces of sound and gravity just keep lashing at her. The air inside smells of ozone. Laika whimpers, then tries to bark, but the noise and the gravity swallow her words. She can see nothing. She cannot even open her eyes. Laika believes this is the end. But after what seemed hours, the hammering stops and the horrible weight lifts itself from her back. She rises from the floor until the straps of her harness pull her to a stop. Frightened but released from gravity, she draws long ragged drafts of the stale air that pollutes the capsule.

Two hundred miles away, men huddle together to listen, watch—taking notes, laughing, congratulating one another. Some hope to learn from this mission, others hope only to slap the Americans' faces. One way or the other, learning isn't an essential part of this project. The essential piece is to be sure that the Americans know that Laika is up there.

The Americans know all right. But not about Laika. Not yet.

Laika knows nothing. None of those who spy on her ever speak to her. She knows only the strange blackness of space. When the Americans discover Laika, they call her "Muttnik."

As Laika entered Earth orbit, the second stage of the booster rocket failed to separate completely from the capsule where she lay. So, now the capsule orbits booster down. That is, the booster remains pointed at the Earth, and the capsule window faces the stars. Because of the attached second stage, Laika's tomb is easily seen by people all over the Earth. A star itself, spinning through the empty heavens. We watch.

A tiny window was cut into the lid of Laika's capsule. So she could see as well. But because of the way the rocket booster and payload orbit, Laika never sees the Earth again. She sees only stars— icy needles burning in a black dome. Laika has never seen so many stars. The video camera was mounted near the window above Laika's head. In the photos of her taken from the video camera, Laika lies in her harness with her forelegs crossed and stares out the window, the light of the camera momentarily blinding her. For fifteen minutes out of every 103, the stars vanish and the capsule fills with light. For fifteen minutes out of every 103, Laika imagines someone has come to get her. Of course, no one has.

The gauges continue to pulse, the air remains chemical, and once sunlight, undiluted sunlight, falls through the window at the foot of Gina's bed. But even that isn't enough to lift the weight from her chest, or to lift the wooden fear from me. It is ten days before anyone tells me Gina will likely live. I hadn't asked. So no one volunteered.

The night they drew straws for Gina's parts, the "knee guy" drew the short straw, so he had to go last. Only after the intestine was shortened, after the shoulder was gone, after the back was bolted, after most of what could be done to Gina had been done to her, did he get a crack at her knees.

But before that happens, Gina insists we return to Fort Collins. She is well enough now to leave ICU, and she is sick nearly to death of the hospital in Denver. The "lung guy" has finally managed to wean Gina off the respirator. And she is ready to leave. The "knee guy" in Denver is very disappointed that we are leaving. He really has developed a little love for Gina's knees. He offers to do the surgery at 5:00 a.m. on Saturday before we leave. Gina refuses. He reluctantly recommends a "knee guy" in Fort Collins, and we leave for home. Not together. She leaves in an ambulance. I leave with my sister and her husband. It is December now, but the sun is shining. After all the darkness, the sun is shining. That, of course, will change.

A day or so after we arrive at the hospital in Fort Collins, we meet another "back guy." He has been chosen for us by someone we do not yet know to follow up on the work begun by the "back guy" in Denver. From the moment we meet, this "back guy" makes it clear he has little interest in and even less time for following up on another "back guy's" work. Gina's back is not her own. Her back belongs to a nameless surgeon in Denver, though she must bear it.

From a distance, the new guy looks at Gina's back, suggests some new X-rays, and without ever touching Gina, he leaves.

The next day, Gina and I meet the new "shoulder guy." He shows up late one evening, still wearing his ski clothes. Tall. Solidly built. Darkly handsome. He holds her chart while he sits in a green plastic chair. Legs crossed. Shoulders slack. Absorbed in his thoughts as water is absorbed by cotton underwear.

"Doctor, I've had no physical therapy for my shoulder. None. I'm worried about that."

"People like you don't rehab well from surgery like this. Oddly enough, you're too young."

"You know, I really wish you wouldn't begin by pigeon-holing me with averages. All I want is to work as hard as I can to bring my shoulder as far as I can. Let's not have any preconceived notions."

"I'll order the physical therapy." He shrugs.

The end.

He never touched her shoulder and he never ordered the physical therapy. People like Gina don't rehab well. He just wanted out of the room.

Once during the next three weeks, a therapist (apparently on her own) offers to help Gina. She shows Gina how to do things Gina didn't think she could do. And she shows her exercises that might help Gina's arm. Gina is so appreciative she cries and holds the technician's hand for as long as she can. Finally, we insist that we see the "shoulder guy" again. He agrees to meet with us on Christmas Eve.

He doesn't come. Later we learn, he changed his mind at the last minute and went skiing with his family. The room distorts around Gina's bed. The white sheets wrinkle and redden. The pale green walls fold in on themselves. Gina would not get her shoulder back, he figured, no matter how much attention he gave it. So he gave it none.

The hallways lengthened and narrowed. The overhead lights turned yellow. I looked at other people now with the eyes of a hare—fearful, jealous. The darkness came again.

Gina's shoulder then did something no one had ever imagined it would. It began making bone. At first that seemed good. But then it didn't stop. Her shoulder went on making bone. And not just shoulder bones, not just scapula and humerus. It began making bone everywhere. "Heterotopic ossification." Bone grew over the top of her shoulder and into the plastic and steel of her prosthesis. Bone grew down her deltoid and into her trapezius. A hard milky cap formed almost overnight and sealed forever beneath its opalescence the handsome young doctor's predictions. But it wasn't, as he had forecast, her youth that took her arm, it was calcium and cartilage and confusion that robbed her. Something no one thought could happen.

When we finally meet with the "shoulder guy" again, we confront the surgeon with his absence. He resents our confrontation.

"These things don't work well in people of your age. They just don't," he spits at us. Watching as Gina struggles to lift her left arm.

"I never asked you for any sort of guarantee." Gina.

"That's not the point." Him.

"These things don't work well in people your age. We all knew that!" Him.

"I never asked for a guarantee that this would work out." Gina.

Finally, me to him:

"You never even said, 'I'll do my best to see to it that things turn out as well as possible.' You never once said you were sorry about what had happened and you would do all you could."

Pause.

Pause.

"I'm sorry," he said.

"I guess we'll find ourselves another physician."

"I understand," he said.

He understood nothing.

Near the end, Laika understands. Everyone has abandoned her. That is clear now. No one will come with the light. But why? She remembers little of the days at Baikonur. She barked a lot, of course. That was only because she was frightened at first. That doesn't seem so terrible. But here she is here alone, her own filth clotted in her fur. The stink of urine, and the heat. It must have been something she did. How else could she explain this? And it must have been something so terrible, so unforgivable that the men who had been so kind to her, who had fed her and played with her, no longer wished to even to speak to her, to touch her, to be anywhere near her. It hurt her to imagine she had done something that so angered these men.

Something that bad, it seemed, she should remember. And she tried. But even when she tried very hard, she could not recall what it was. All of them had seemed so nice, so anxious to make her feel important. How could she have been so stupid?

"I'd be friggin' depressed too."

Gina's out of the hospital now and these words are from the new (third) "shoulder guy." This guy isn't really a "shoulder guy," he's sort of a "knee guy." Only he doesn't do knees like Gina's. He was the best the hospital could find after we fired "shoulder guy" number two. Number three is explaining to Gina why she should take antidepressants. To encourage her, he is explaining that he certainly would take antidepressants if he were anywhere near as fucked up as she is. This is what is known as bedside manner.

We're at a clinic in Fort Collins. Gina has struggled onto an examining table. I'm sitting in a chair on lifts, little blocks of wood under the chair's legs. I don't know what the lifts are for. The doctor is wearing his labcoat. I'm thinking I should have worn mine. The overhead light is thinking nothing at all, I guess. A bottle full of tongue depressors and a box of Kleenex watch us from the counter top.

"I've known lots of people who got along just fine with a completely fused shoulder. "It isn't your arm that's the problem. It's your head. Get over it—that's what you should do. I feel good about this already. You need an antidepressant."

Gina isn't so certain. After all, it is her arm, regardless of what she has been told.

"What about options for my shoulder?" she says, tearing up.

"I'd be afraid I'd make it worse. People your age don't do well with these prostheses, and I might make it worse. I think you're just going to have to accept that this is the way it's going to be for someone your age.

"What about rehab?"

"If it hurts, I wouldn't do it. Your shoulder is not going to get any better. But, I'll talk to a colleague. A "shoulder guy" I know in New York. Get his thoughts about all of this."

Of course, he won't. I've become cynical.

Gina, though, seems a little encouraged.

What "shoulder guy number three" did do, regularly, was pass whatever information we gave him onto the other "shoulder guy," the one we fired. "Semi-shoulder guy number three" would then simply pass back to us whatever "originally fired-shoulder guy number two" told him about Gina's shoulder. Neither number two or number three ever touched her shoulder.

After all, it wasn't their shoulder to begin with. Just whose shoulder it was, no one knew for certain. But though it probably wasn't truly Gina's shoulder, it was time for her to get used to it. Everyone agreed on that.

"Take the antidepressant, and maybe you should try some Oxycodone as well. I'll present your case at rounds next Friday to see what all the specialists here think about this. But I don't have much hope for surgery. I think the antidepressant is the answer. I feel good about that. I'll leave a prescription at the front desk."

None of these were even his ideas. All of it—the opinions, the prescriptions, the pain killers, the antidepressants, the gloomy forecasts, and all the shitty advice—was still coming to us from the man we told to get out of our lives. This man, the one in front of us, is just the go-between. And the advice we are given is still filled up with the wisdom of averages and the commitment of the bored.

Gina begins to cry seriously. The doctor walks out. She'd rehearsed her story for two weeks before this meeting. The story she would tell them about who she was and how hard she would work, how proud she could make them if they would just give her a chance. But no one ever asked her to tell her story. No one ever gave her a chance. No one. Now there are only her tears—rainwater up from the sea.

Indifference has ensnared us within its tepid arms. Gina's shoulder is forfeit. Next it will be her knees.

The air is nearly gone now, Laika knows that. Each breath is harder to draw and hold. She can't stop panting. It is so hot here. Less than seven days in orbit, and her support systems are failing. The coolers are no longer working properly and the oxygen generator is going as well. She has never been this frightened in her life. The men on Earth know what's happening to Laika, but they cannot tell her. Besides, the scientists have accomplished what they wished anyway, even in so few days. Days full of night. Days full of stars. Days full of failure. There is no need for more.

The last of the oxygen bleeds into the cabin and into Laika. She settles as best she can in her harness and the weightlessness of her capsule. Confusion pushes every other thought from her mind. The burning in her lungs slows and finally stops. Unforgiven, her heart simply quits pumping. Her last thought is of food.

Six months later, Laika's corpse burns to black ash when her ship reenters the Earth's upper atmosphere, slams against the fierce wall of air the dog once so loved to breathe. Fire and ice. A streak of flame cracks the darkness over the northern hemisphere as she hurtles across the sky. Then there is only silence and darkness and ash.

The light scatters. We gather it again, focus the rays with the lenses left to us. Images rise. But nothing is as it was. Nothing.

Such a Deal

There once was a man who wanted to be a writer. Sometimes he would sit for as long as an hour at his desk with a spiral notebook and a number-two pencil and stare at the blank white page and dream of filling it with words. But no words came to him. Often he would doodle, making circles and squares that intersected in bewildering patterns. It was a maze which he couldn't find any way out of. He filled whole pages in this way. On bad days he couldn't even create a new doodle. He would trace and retrace an old one, making it heavier and heavier until the page was a mass of shadows. But he knew that a shadow was not a story. Then he would chew on his pencil until it was reduced to a pile of splinters, his teeth were black with graphite, and pink eraser crumbs clung to his lips. He looked as if he had been to a banquet for starving artists.

In his youth he had been a devout Roman Catholic, but he had grown bored and left the church when he realized that the priest kept telling the same stories year after year. They were always about fishing with nets from small boats, working in vineyards, and rescuing sheep. He had looked for new stories, first in bottles of sour-mash Bourbon, which he had purchased with a fake ID, then in marijuana, which he grew in his bathroom and dried in his kitchen. When he was high, he thought how easy it would be to become a writer, but when he came down, he could make nothing of the visions he had received.

One midnight in July he sat at his desk in the living room of his apartment and traced a doodle that he had made the previous week. Through his open window a faint, warm breeze blew the sound of a clock chime, and it reminded him of the bells that had announced Mass when he was a child. The breeze freshened, and a sudden gust slapped him across the face with the lace curtain. It made him recall the sleeve of a priest's vestment and being embraced. He found himself wondering if prayer would help. "What the hell," he said, "why not?"

The next Sunday he was in the back pew of Sisters of the Cross and Passion Roman Catholic Church attending eleven o'clock Mass.

As soon as he discovered that the priest's stories were unchanged, he paid no attention to the service. While others knelt to pray, stood to sing, or sat to hear the lesson for the day, he remained on his knees. While the rest murmured prescribed responses to the litany which the priest recited, he made up his own prayer and flung it squarely at his maker. "Please, God," he said, "I want to be a writer."

And to his amazement God whispered into his ear. "I am thy shepherd, thou shalt...."

And the man interrupted with his own whisper into God's ear. "I know, I know. I don't mean to be rude, but I've heard that one. Frankly, I've had it up to here with that sheep metaphor."

And God said, "Let me give you a little tip, Mister. If you want folks to listen to you, don't whine so much. And while we're talking here, how about some praise for the Almighty? Better yet, how about a little charity? Think about somebody other than yourself for Christ's sake! . . . and I say that reverently."

The prayer rail was harder than the man had remembered. He shifted his whole weight to his left knee. "Bless me, Father, for I have sinned. It has been ten years since my last confession. I..."

And God interrupted, "Spare me. Don't you think I'd like to hear a new story, too? This is just the same old same old. Everybody wants to make a deal. But what you got here is half a deal. What's in it for the Kingdom of the Lord (if you'll excuse the old-fashioned, feudal, patriarchal metaphor)?"

So the man imagined himself making God rich for sweet charity's sake at 10% of all royalties, movie studio option, screenplay advance, consultant fee, plus 3% of box office gross, royalties and residuals from after market video and dvd sales as well as product spin offs—T-shirts, coffee mugs, video games, happy-meal plastic toys. In this way he invented his first story, a fantastic tale with himself as the protagonist and God Almighty as his patron, his chief investor, his angel. And although the man didn't know what he was doing, as he emerged from his reverie at the end of the service, he saw the priest's right hand waving above the congregation like it was writing invisible words in the air. The man thought this was a good sign.

That evening just after dark, the man sat at his desk doodling.

He found himself making more circles than squares. Then on a whim he added a cross to the top of one circle. When he looked up from his notebook and out the window of his apartment, he saw a brilliant white flash on his fire escape and heard the sound of wings like a thousand chickens had come home to roost. An angel folded her wings, hiked up silken robes around her thighs and ducked in through his open window. She stood beside his desk and smiled down at him the way Mia Farrow had looked at Robert Redford in The Great Gatsby. "Jesus Christ!" he said. "This prayer shit really works!"

The angel spread her wings and steepled her fingers. "Behold the Angel of the Lord. Blessed art thou among men, for thou shall conceive and bring forth a book, and it shall be called IT'S A MIRACLE. And thou shalt be famous."

And the man said, "Reeeeally? Tell me how!"

And the angel replied, "A beautiful muse shall appear to thee and lie with thee and make thy mind fruitful, and thou shall write for nine months without ceasing and then thou shalt bring forth the great story. Of course, there is some pain and travail in there owing to the labor involved."

Suddenly the man realized his buttocks had fallen asleep. He squirmed, "Nine months. That's a long time. How about weekends off?"

The angel smiled shrewdly. "That's not part of the deal. So stop whining. I've got the contract right here. Sign it, Mister, or go fish."

He signed.

"The yellow one is your copy," she said sweetly, folding the original and inserting it in the flap pocket of her left wing. "Enjoy, but don't forget your part of the deal. You warrant that you will deposit cash only in the collection box of any denomination Christian Church or Jewish Synagogue 10% of any payments received by you, excluding, of course, your initial cash advance for startup costs. Further, you acknowledge that interest accrues on any portion of late payments at 18.7 % per month based upon an average daily balance which will be calculated for you by God. I know it sounds like usury, but that's the prevailing credit-card rate. And He doesn't like to take unfair advantage of His position vis a vis market conditions." She hiked up her robes. "Say, I don't suppose there's any way I can get up to the roof, is there? These fire escapes are okay to land on, but they're a bitch for take-offs."

The man shook his head sadly. Then, he stood at the window and watched as the angel fell into a steep, graceless dive. At the last second she managed enough lift to clear the gravel and tar roof of the Midtown Deli; then she disappeared behind the blackened brick chimney over Mel's Tailor Shop.

The next evening after dinner the man heard a knock at his door. When he opened it, he saw a Black woman tall enough to play power forward in the WNBA. Her hair was in dreadlocks with red, white, and blue beads separating the strands. Her purple eye shadow matched her lipstick and nail polish. She wore no bra beneath the black, sleeveless tank top. Her black leather mini-skirt stopped at mid thigh. The tops of her black vinyl boots disappeared beneath the skirt. She smelled strongly of musk oil.

The man said, "Yes?"

She looked him up and down slowly. "In my business, Baby, that's the good word. Now shift that out the interrogative mood, throw in some moanin' and groanin,' and you on your way to bein' a writer for Shady Grove Press."

The man was stunned. "So, you are...."

"I your Muse, Baby. I be here to aaaaaa-muse." She burst into a wild raucous laugh that reminded him of a flock of crows.

He found her seductive but not what he had imagined. He wondered: What is God up to? He wanted time to reconsider what he was getting himself into. So, slowly the man began to ease the door closed. "You can't come in right now. It's not convenient. Uh... I've got a pot boiling on the stove," he lied. "Come later."

She looked down at him and cocked her right hip. "You just nervous, Baby. Everybody nervous they first time."

He stalled, "I, um, have to phone my agent. I, ah, need to check my contract. You come some other time."

She planted her right foot on the threshold and pushed her knee against his door. "You wanta be a writer or not? 'Cause you might talk like a writer, but you ain't one yet, else I wouldn't a got sent over here." Suddenly she ran her left hand up under her skirt. "I got what you need, Baby. I'm reeeeal good at makin' somethin' big outta somethin' little. Like the white bitch say, 'if you cain't do that, you ain't gonna amount to much as a writer.'" She looked pointedly at his crotch. It didn't seem promising.

"White bitch? What white bitch? You mean the Angel of the Lord?

"Naw, course not! You ain't never heard a Flannery O'Connor, Baby? You ain't read *Mystery and Manners?* If you gonna be a writer, you gots to read more."

"I know, I know. Just come back later. I need to, you know, get ready." And with that he swept her aside and shut the door.

The man turned around and fell to his knees. The floor was white oak. It hurt like the devil. Suddenly he knew how it felt to be James Brown. He began to pray. "Please, God, I want to renegotiate. I want to be famous, not notorious. I can't consort with a muse right off the streets. It's too much too soon. She's not my type. She's too colorful."

And God spoke to the man, "Consort, huh? That's a new word you learned already! Now listen up. You want to be a writer, you need to think outside the box. I'm asking you straight out: You got something against Black folks?"

And the man felt silent for what seemed like centuries. Finally he said "It's hard to be sure, but I really don't think so."

And God said, "That sounds like an honest answer. You know, when I read *The Turner Diaries,* it made me ashamed to have invented language and to have given human beings the power of speech. So, you can take this to the bank: I am not getting into the business of underwriting a racist novel! And if that's where you're headed with this, I'm breaking our contract under section three, paragraph five, bullet one!"

The man raised his head a little higher. "Okay. Okay, then. Point well taken and understood. But what about vocabulary? What about style? Don't you think she's too much Muse for me! I'm a beginner here. Think about my...ah...comfort level." He scratched his butt.

"So what kind of muse suits you, Mr. Particular?"

And the man lifted up his eyes in amazement, "You're Jewish?"

And God laughed just like Buddy Hackett. "My only begotten Son was Jewish. Sometimes I'm Jewish. So what, then, you were expecting, Irish?"

"Well, yes, or maybe Italian."

And God said, "You want to talk stereotypes? Somebody already wrote *The Godfather* also *The Barrytown Trilogy*. So, now all of a sudden you don't want to make a deal because I'm Jewish?"

"No, no, of course not. I was just surprised. I want to go through with it. We just need to clarify the terms."

And God said, "So talk. I'll listen."

"God," he said, "I need something exotic, not pornographic; something stylish, not flashy; something classy, not pushy."

And God said, "That's some prose rhythm you got working there, Kiddo. All right, all right. You think you know best? Have it your way. Man! Saul Bellow I didn't have this much trouble with. And you I'm warning. Anymore *kvetching,* Mister, and you'll be working for *The National Inquirer*. You'll be chasing stretch limos. You'll be doing a piece on the President's putz.

The man lifted up his eyes and beheld a brilliant white light streaming through the transom above his door. Immediately he heard knocking. Heaving himself up off his battered knees, he limped to the door, and opened it a crack. He saw the face of the Angel of the Lord who had appeared to him, and he threw open his door. She was without wings and clothed in a navy blue tropical wool Donna Karan suit, nylons, and high heels. Her makeup was so subtle as to be invisible: A light rose blush on her cheeks, pale pink gloss on her lips, no eye shadow. Her right hand held a buttery leather attaché case. She smelled faintly of jasmine. As a would-be writer, the man had imagined that he would know what he needed when he saw it. He was looking at it now.

He took a step forward. "You again? Thank God!"

She held her ground. "Just between us girls, there's been a little downsizing up...." and gestured with her blue eyes toward heaven. "I'm moonlighting." She smiled and tossed her wavy blond hair. It floated. "In fact, I just got the call. Tonight I'm the Doubleday Muse.

May I come in?"

"You bet," the man said, and followed her into his apartment, grateful that he had made his bed.

On a beautiful spring Saturday afternoon nine months later the man sat squirming at his desk. He had been laboring steadily, and now it seemed about to pay off. But making a book had been a host of troubles. Perched on the edge of the chair for eight hours everyday, his buttocks seemed to have gone permanently numb as if he had been administered a series of spinal blocks. His belly was as round as a globe; the burden of the thirty five pounds he had gained strained against his Sansabelt slacks. His wrists were swaddled in leather braces so that he could keep pecking away at the keyboard of his Macintosh IBook even with carpal-tunnel syndrome. And when he peered down at the computer screen, it was through a pair of horn-rimmed glasses with lenses thick as the bottom of a Hellman's mayonnaise jar. They magnified everything and gave him a splitting headache. He pulled back his right hand, groped the trackpad, and pulled down the file menu. He clicked the print command and sighed as his Hewlett Packard Deskjet 5550 began to deliver the manuscript of *IT'S A MIRACLE* at seventeen pages per minute. The man giggled with anticipation, imagining himself a famous author featured on The Oprah Winfrey Show. Suddenly he discovered that by raising one cheek and then the other, he was able to rub some feeling back into his tired butt. Miraculously his headache was disappearing. He felt thinner by the minute.

One gray April morning a year later the writer sat at his desk looking through a thick folder of reviews. Thunder rumbled over the rooftops. The black enamel fire escape looked dangerously slippery. The heavens had opened up. Literary critics had loved *It's a Miracle*. Oprah Winfrey had selected it for her book club. But he was depressed. There had been no royalties, and he had been forced to return his modest cash advance to the publisher. Hollywood had declined optioning it for a screenplay. An executive with International Creative Management in Burbank had told him brusquely: "Too much dialog; too few explosions. Too much love; not enough sex." The novel had sold only fifteen hundred copies—not even enough to cover printing costs. His agent would not return his phone calls. And Oprah was stunned. Her imprimatur on *It's a Miracle* had not made it an instant best seller. *The National Inquirer* had reported that she was rumored to be in therapy over her apparent inability to improve the reading taste of her otherwise devoted followers.

Except for his desk and chair, there was practically no furniture left in the writer's apartment. All his appliances had been sold, replaced by a hot plate, paper plates, and plastic utensils sitting on a sagging card table in the corner. He had given up his day job with Xerox and eaten his way through the apartment. Frankly, he was puzzled. How could God grace him with talent that touched the hardest critic's heart and yet allow him to fail so dramatically in the market place? Was it too much to ask that God Almighty elevate the literary taste of every man, woman, and child in the United States of America? Was God testing his commitment to his new vocation? There was a knock at the door, a hollow sound that echoed through his study.

When the writer opened it, he saw the Doubleday Muse. She looked as sweet and innocent as she had on the night they had spent together. She smiled broadly and held out a copy of *It's a Miracle*. "I found this on the remainder table at Barnes and Noble. I know it is not everybody's thing, but I loved it. In fact, I saw a piece of me in it," she gushed. "May I have your autograph?"

"Of course," the writer said. "I appreciate your asking." But when he opened his book to the first blank page, the old sense of lethargy seized him. He felt the impulse to doodle, to fill it with circles and squares and shadows. Then, he remembered he had become a writer. He removed a number two pencil from behind his ear and scrawled "thanks for the memories." Then he signed his name with a professional flourish, putting so much body English into it that he nearly threw his back out.

"Thank you," she purred and kissed him on the lips chastely. She gestured toward his apartment. "May I?"

"Of course," the writer said and stood aside to let her in.

As soon as she had slipped past him, she removed her raincoat, then her skirt and blouse. As he watched, he thought about his second novel. He was not sure he could rise to the occasion. He felt exhausted. So, he was relieved when she shook out the white silky robe beneath and unfurled her wings.

She handed him her designer clothing. "Here you go. Consider this old outfit a keepsake. I've got to get back to my day job." Then, tucking *It's a Miracle* into the flap pocket of her left wing, she crossed to the window, opened it, and stepped onto the fire escape.

As the writer turned to close the door, he saw the Shady-Grove-Press Muse leaning against the casement. She wore a cocky smile and a colorful new outfit. It made him realize this was Good Friday. Easter was just around the corner. He saw her hair was covered by a silk turban white as the wing of an Angel of the Lord. Her voluptuous figure was wreathed in a lycra body suit blue as a dyed egg. It left nothing even to his newly fertile imagination. The nylon book bag slumped at her feet sported a bumper sticker plastered above the flap—black script on a white field. It read "slippery when wet."

"Hey, Man," she cooed, "we ain't forget about the rest of that deal. 'Cause ten percent a nothin' for the Kingdom of Heaven is still nothin'. Y'all better be ready to make some reeeeal money this time. God knows you got obligations. And I ain't talkin' IRS. Not yet anyways."

The writer looked her over more carefully this time. She was a complete package all right, not just fancy wrapping as he first imagined. And, after all, hadn't God sent her first? Maybe he needed to have a little more faith in The Almighty. God knows, he thought, I could use the stimulation now. At his back he heard the flutter of wings as the Angel of the Lord took her perilous flight, straining toward the higher altitudes. But he'd been there, done that. "What the hell," he thought. Then the author of *It's a Miracle* stepped aside to usher in the real answer to his prayers.

Shoes

Tough shoes, thick-tongued leather shoes, laced up
tight, not to come undone, how life starts
with babies' first shoes, sponged white & saved
in a clear box or bronzed on a platform, little girls
in calf-skin, kid skin, patent leathers for making First Communion in,
shined with Vaseline, buckled down, the white & brown
saddle shoes of Catholic schools, Buster Browns, Stride Rites,
penny loafers with nickels slipped in; the tasseled, the tied, the wide
Wing Tips of Wall Street, the blue suede shoes of the King,
snakeskin, man-made uppers and rubber soles, old shoes with holes
in soles, can't seem to throw them away, Keds for baby boomer
women seeing themselves in ads, affording designer shoes,
expensive even-on-sale Via Spiga of Italy shoes, Donald J Pliner
shoes handmade in the mountains of Italy, Italians
producing pants that fit & stilettos of lust; got to have the walking shoe,
the airport shoe, the shoe to slip off during love-making, those red shoes,
& the squeaky shoes that say you're arriving, that say you're leaving;
there are shoes that sell cars & shoes that say you're practical,
there are the shoes of stories, delicate pumps filled with champagne,
satin & lace covered fabric shoes dyed to match the dress,
& glass slippers that disappear at midnight, shoes
that bring you home & shoes you don't take off, ruby slippers,
a good pair of Nikes; shoes to walk the dog in, jog in,
new ones to break in, give you rhythm, & shoes that make you tall,
tri-colored platform shoes looking good with tight jeans, shoes
that go with fashion & shoes that make you punk, Greenwich Village
café boots imitating army issue or the thick shoes of the oppressed in Russia;
shoes to Polka as fast as you can in, get a grip in, the Kinney's shoes
Dad tapped danced in, made us kids laugh again, shoes Gene sang
& danced in the rain in, Riverdance, the sound of a cast of shoes
rapping hard on wooden floors, clapping for more, moving our feet,

the sound of the one-heart beat, an uncle, a cop walking the beat,
marching feet in unison, never-out-of-step beat, toe the line
stride in Floresheims; rubber-thonged happy feet, Dunhams
covered in mud, closed-toed shoes to walk through puddles in,
sling backs you're not suppose to walk in puddles with,
Totes to keep the water out, lead boots people have drowned in,
the only pair of new shoes he owned, to bury my brother in;
donated shoes, worn thrift store shoes, markdowns, hand-me-downs,
first pair of heels worn with nylons to church,
feeling like a big girl though-my-feet-ache shoes,
white go-go boots, singing with Nancy, "gonna walk all over you,"
the old woman, who didn't really live in a shoe;
shoes that point, that have a steel toe, 5 ½—my size,
grandpa's prize fighting, dodging shoes; don't have the right shoes,
the shoes that match, don't match, kids in India without shoes,
Jellies for the beach, sand in shoes, "made in America"
billboard shoes that didn't last, orthopedic shoes,
extra-wide-width shoes, old lady shoes & widow Red Cross shoes,
time & time again the empty shoes, the hollows
filled with shoe trees or ecru paper, the thrown away shoe,
the mud-caked, left-on-the-riverbank shoes, the army issue
of the unknown soldier, the one shoe lost under the bed;
my new black boots, better than any shoes,
look like the spit-shined Navy boots my father wore,
his coming-home boots, tight-on-the-heel boots,
felt them with my whole body pulling, slip off,
fall to the floor.

Twelve Days from Transfer

Because they suppress you with Lupron & that's the easy-to-mix
shot, the cheapest shot, the thinnest diabetic's needle that goes
into the soft part of the belly, hell, that one you can give
to yourself with a running start, in airport bathrooms, friends'
bedrooms, wherever you're going, this one won't slow you down
on day 21.

Because 50% of follicles contain an egg, they build you up
with Metroden, FSH, 30-40 amps per cycle, $2,000 of the $12,000
you'll spend & this is where you need to totally trust
someone to break the glass ampoules cleanly & mix the white tablets
with 2cc's of saline & clear the syringes of air bubbles
without losing even a drop, to put their hand on your butt
in the shape of an L & find the corner of skin where your top
pocket would be so they don't hit a nerve & inject the 1½-
inch needle into the muscle.

Because they tell you not to worry, the symptoms are temporary,
you take the headaches, hot flashes, vaginal dryness, bruising
at the injection site, abdominal bloating, breast tenderness,
moodiness & irritability.

Because they check you every other morning, then every morning
at 7:30 a.m., take blood, do a vaginal ultrasound & you see
your follicles like gray moons on a screen, mapped by x's,
intern of the day calling out the numbers to record on a sheet until
there are some 13 on the left ovary & at least 10 on the right,
over 18mm averages & he'll smile as he says, "Tonight might be
the night," & you actually look forward to HCG, Profasi
or Pregnyl, the toughest shot for side effects, but he says,
"We'll call you when we have your estradiol."

Because HCG matures follicles, retrieval is 34 hours after
injection & Dr. Jones, IVF clinic, does a transvaginal oocyte
aspiration using a probe attached to a suction pump & they get
9 eggs, great for a 41-year-old woman.

Because they give you the dish from the fertilized embryos
as a souvenir & you see them on the screen, their cells
divided so they are no longer zygotes, their outer shell
intact, they all look good, perfect even & you want to
name them lying there on the table, rolling dice
in your mind, give the OK, let's put in 6.

Because they support you with progesterone suppositories
& Estraderm patches, the lining of your uterus builds & you
become full, there is no other way to explain it & in 12 days
you know if you're pregnant.

Because 12 days is a long time to wait & you don't
want the lab to take blood anymore, nick your hemorrhagic
veins, wait for estradiol levels or follicular sizes
& the speculations of the best doctors as to what is
your next best shot & you don't want to open
your legs for the vaginal ultrasound microphone
covered by a rubber & cold, sea green gel before you
even have your breakfast, have sex on the right day, at
the right hour, whether you want to or not, be home
at 7 p.m. to pull down your pants, & Jesus
to talk about it & no, you don't want to try this again.

The Fair Shulamite, the Shekinah

She comes with coins tinkling,
    a musical bodice.
She comes with perfume and peace:
    from the foot of a sacred mountain,
    from the lofty mount of transfiguration.
She fills his tents with peace.
    He writes 1000 and five songs.
She dances and the wind cools.
    He conquers the desert.
She is the shadow of our tribe:
    the one haunting her eyes,
    the shadow of understanding.
She need not strike or stroke,
    the bargain-sealer rises each dawn.
She roots and flowers.
She falls with water,
    lifts as thermals,
        blazes.
She is round-edged sand,
    carving mountains.
She springs from cleft stone.
She has feet of a gazelle.
    She has eyes of an ibex.
        She has hips of a wild ass.
    She has the smile of a camel.
She has the voice of a naqla dove.
She tunes my harp.
    She cooks with dates.
        She speaks in tongues.
She comes with premonitions,
    in her dreams each night.
She brings her own wealth.

She causes him to shake.
        He wants to bow down to her.
She transmutes his fear.
        He washes her offering
        and prays with its flame.
He may be beloved of God
        and invent 3000 proverbs,
        but she is a gift, a grace.
See, she comes with gold coins shimmering.

Driving Highway 19, Through Osceola's Forest With Nancy

For Nancy Bennett and Marjorie Kinnan Rawlings

Where we always stop, pit stop, there's
a kiosk, with boiled peanuts (sometimes shrimp) and gas
from ultramodern singing commercial tanks, O
all the modern conveniences, and a clean
ladies', besides. We talk of bowling.
(She's my Captain.) hopeful. Lately we're not
very victorious, but it's tournament time
and we're cautiously, what'd I say?
hopeful.

This is Osceola's forest, and in the station now
hunters gather in camouflage jackets, khakis, to buy Cokes
and the specialty, fried chicken. Smell those floating
globules of fat, the sizzle, as chicken skin crisps.
Their boots trample, cadent, in line.
O yes. Lottery tickets.

In the forest, there's a sign—
an arrow (all traces of Osceola only in imagination, shining
greasy-pigtailed visions that flicker through palmettos
live oak holly bay and dogwood) to PAT'S ISLAND.
Red birds, maybe. Red birds and green orange groves—
nowhere near deep water. Only marshes. "An 'Island,'
I tell Nancy, "Is a hammock. A stand of pine
and this is called 'The Scrub'" —dreaming
Sink Hole, bear and feisty dog, and the young boy's grief.

They shot *The Yearling* here."
Sounding like a teacher again. Disgusting.
Dreaming deer, and foxes. Lob lolly. Cedars
and cypress knees, brownedged magnolia leaves—

the scent is turpentine. "Ummm," says Nancy.
"Maybe we should wear our own shirts
And forget the team's."

THE GRASSHOPPER

is
legs all tendon, set to spring
le gras hopp-aire

O, leap.

Don't just sit there
palpitating
bug

or, is
crème de menthe, crème de cacao
and rich cow's cream
shattered together

across ice

tongue between lips, O
slush

or, me

flic, flic, the same
blade to grass or lip to glass
O, leap!

Can't hover here forever
hungering

Love.

LOSS

Though I have lost mother, some memory,
    a camera with film, dark pieces of Oregon inside,
numerous coins, pens, points—there is no loss.

Although the violin disintegrates in the swamp
    and the cobbled path to the Mayan cenote
is missing a few round notes, there is no loss.

It seems there is loss because I know nothing more
    of Judy whom I half-loved, or a favorite teacher
who is dead, or the umbrella I left in Portugal

but there is no loss because my teacher's
    loved comedian in the '50s, George Gobel,
is also dead, and because Judy surely has lost

an umbrella at least once in her life. It feels
    like loss, those opposite landscapes of film
I'll never recognize, and it feels like loss,

the photographs I can't name the place of
    or am dumb about the year, and here
is one I know: the title of the ornate church,

even the date of that blue sunshine,
    though not the woman in a red scarf
moving away at the left, head lowered.

But Judy, this is the amazing thing,
    walks this moment in a city—
moving away to the left and it's not raining—

neither thinking of loss nor certainly of me,
  looking forward to something small
which makes her smile and then, further amused

to realize she is smiling, smile more
  and no one around her notices
this moment and nothing is ever lost.

Reading the Suicide Trees

From inside out, this
thriving elm
snuffs its own cells; cortex
thickens, branches spread.
Crush a leaf, and it weeps.

Some say walls around a heart
can't heal. I disagree.
Harvested bark yields
spices, fibers. Medicines,
resins—death every minute

brings gifts. A friend
bathed his dying mother's feet.
Cupped layers of skin, coming
away—and more than that—
adhered to his dripping hands.

When bark fails, no elm
survives. Stored, silent
in those leaves, the light
ebbs, and the used rain
passes away.

The Taken

Now your life begins to change
forever, though not in ways you
recognize at first or even notice.
A stormy dawn's hectic organza;
frost's smoky palette darkening
to pencil-point among the chaste
utensils of the stricken groves: So
days and nights secure the sullen,
silken knot of increase and erosion,
and your patience and your sorrow
would fill a valley of bright marble
with black water. How perfect, how
reasonable to cede no inch of your
allegiance to the dreamed of, the
sought for and lost; the tempted,
the promised,
the taken.

Discerning only...

Discerning only that the dead are dead,
I am not prepared for their resurrection:
the daily, the bread, the fine lines on their
hands and wrinkled faces. No one has longed
for this solitude, begged endless nights
for its skeletal angles, the coins on its eyes,
its burden of dawning, suspended balance.

A helicopter roars low over the river, hovers,
disappears in mist. The dead are castigating
our neglect, filling archives of accusation
with their insatiate hunger. Take them at
their word, take the why, the wry hand
of a partner. Only the first step requires blood.

You are leaving late, packed but unprepared,
carrying the scarred suitcase of self, battered
by age, you thought you'd trashed years ago.
We learn slowly and as from the beginning
how to live, in the middle reaches of a life,
near its end. Or never. The fear of death
and the fear of life are twins with nothing
in common. Anguished or ecstatic, we
crave finality's foretaste: a sop, a breast.

Notes

The sky is an empty bowl, the light
something I turn away from. My son
is in Boston this morning. I don't know
if he's as happy in love as he was. Does he?
In a dream just before the alarm wakes me,
a man emptying a dishwasher puts pieces
of paper away with the dishes, notes
about who each piece of silver or glass
or china reminds him of. My life is like
the glasses this man is putting away, fragile
yet clear container of past and present, full
of signs of the people in it. Everywhere
shafts of language open into our lives.
A friend tells me how strange her husband
seems with his father; another, that his son's
therapist said the child has the self-esteem
of an ant. Separating, parents find they have
divorced their children, not their shared past.
I cannot give up the trappings of motherhood,
my husband those of fatherhood. Love and
alienation are names defining the possible,
a world of interiors, artificial as all our homes.
No one moves freely in their gardens, rooms,
corridors, the spaces of art and order we've
created. We enter them trailing remnants
of bondage, old woes, the stories
and children of suffering.

Salsify

"born in the infinite disorder of prayers"
—*Andre Breton*

We are undisciplined, of smaller mind,
the white sun multiplied and gone to seed.
Wind, raise us up
like china plates from the suds.
Raise us up with your own brand of rinsing.
The tiny purple grains trail
from shocks of timothy. Breast feathers
are plucked from the thistle,
and our strange globes, each
isolate, appear,
not all-at-once like dandelions in the field.
The trees are perfect. They remember
their color, the correct order of its will.
Black birch turns butter and lingers,
the alder blackens, and curls.
Then one cloud tears itself from the southeast
and here, the others follow.
In sleep, small birds will tighten their claws
and drift, leaving their bodies to the world.
The fish dreams, a steadying
out of the current.
Once, we were yellow, emblematic,
marked by the bright slivers of our bloom.
To get from that to this, we must be
unafraid of the small expansions of emptiness.
We must billow, knot, and take the rack.
We, who are a collection
of old sayings, all with the same message:
detach. Detach, feel the tug

at your scalp. A yard light glows from the top
of its stalk and finds its way
into the darkest crooks of the field.
What do we know of the immanent good?
We have feathers
and the rough-scaled anchor of seeds. Seeds?
Not now. Bless this time
when we desist, apostate and distracted,
eluding the rough edges of our end.

THE ATOMIC ARK

The boat climbs out of the water, inserts itself next to the barn.
The farmer can hardly see, his glasses thick and icy, even in the
heat. His wife fills with voices. Cows, a few horses, chickens,
pigs, and ducks. But mostly goats and baggy sheep. It is 1946,
and the boat loaded with the animals withdraws, sets sail for
the South Pacific. Because the farmer cannot see, his wife
points him in the direction of the boat, and they wave goodbye,
mystified, flattened in the heat.

She reminds herself
of the handshadows

she casts on the wall of her bedroom at night,

knowing
her husband cannot see them.

It is 1946, and the boat arrives in the South Pacific. Back on the
farm, what is left of the farmer's eyes burns out of his head
eventually. All he does is pray for rain, endless, cleansing rain.
All day the woman tends to the constant flow of milk from
breasts. All night she arranges for the copulations in the barns,
in the straw, in the fields. It is 1946, and the military punctually
detonates an atomic blast above the boat loaded with goats and
sheep.

They call   the experiment

The Atomic Ark.

A terrible noise

scrapes across the sky. And then a terrible quiet.

NIGGER

The father

brought home the word

nigger

and laid it on the kitchen table
with his handcuffs and his badge.

A prison guard, he would explain how they would take the civil rights demonstrators from booking to the cells. In the elevator they would beat them good. It wasn't clear from his description whether he threw any punches.

"You don't know how hard

I tried

to have another father."

He brought home

a silence slash sermon;

it filled up the house

with two hundred years.

I tried to explain it with sociology, psychology, history. I watched things die around my father's hands. He once showed me how to subdue a prisoner. He once showed me how to hit so you wouldn't leave any bruises. Once a man escaped from my father. Being taken from a holding cell to a courtroom, the prisoner got away. The father was never the same. Humiliation collapsed inside his throat.

After Malcom X
and Martin Luther King,
            after a decade of token change,

in a room stuffed with TV-silence.

It was after the divorce, after the children stopped visiting him, after he was diagnosed with throat cancer. He bought a parrot and kept it in a cage. I don't know what words he tried to teach it, but the parrot never said anything. It just sat green and purple in its cage with golden bars as thin as tear ducts. After the father died, his sheriff's patches, like flattened hearts, the ones he wore on the sleeves of his uniform, were shoved in with all his other stuff.

"He once showed me how to hit

so you wouldn't leave

any bruises.

But now I know that's absolutely impossible."

I've seen the documentaries—the courage it took to cross a
bridge against dogs and batons and firehoses. The courage to sit
on a bus or at a lunch counter in Woolworth's. The courage to
be a man, to be a woman. To be a man, to be a woman. I want
to say to the person who stumbles out of the elevator: Tell me
my father didn't do this to you. Tell me it was anyone. Tell me it
was me—my 200 years of cowardice.

This green and purple thing

that slumps inside me.
     Silent and afraid.

"You don't know how hard I tried to have another father."

peace valley elementary school during the vietnam war

I could've been anyone

the three black kids in the whole school at the time
      whom no one else played with at recess—

the girl so embarrassed to exist
      her eyes slid sideways whenever you talked to her,
      or the pretty blonde who liked the smart boys
      and who could afford to sympathize with anyone—

the one who smiled equally at us all,
      the janitor married to the 4th grade teacher
      in bad plaid dresses, greasy gray hair,
      a stooping gait and a bulldozer face—

the 5th grade teacher who loved reading
      after-recess stories to us,
      stroking our damp heads on wood desktops,
      her voice smooth like her fingers,
      her book a lantern held slightly before her—

the tall oaks hemming the field
      that whistled and hissed shrill in the hurricane—

the mouse that bit the boy at Show and Tell
      triggering so much rage he yelled, *"You bastard!"*
      then ran outside, his clenched-white fist
      flinging it to the asphalt—

the big white splash the mouse made
in the frothing thundershower
stunning everyone—

or that boy's friend who raced right after him
half to stop the killing and half just to get soaked!

or the Texan we teased for being short:
"Ah thought evrathing frum Texuz wuz BIG!"

the 2nd grade girl only I would like
because I couldn't see her "cooties"
and she didn't see my color—

the 2nd grade teacher with a face all smooth,
her hair all light,
her voice like singing
until her navy man returned for her;
like a flower unstrung from the sun
she cried and clung ecstatic
against his unyielding uniform,
its blue the darkest we ever saw,
his aura raw like the war—

the kid whose right hand didn't work, "Lefty,"
who was left out of games till the only other choice
was Barry the smelly fat kid—

or Barry's sister who dressed "weird," he said
with a leer that mired the air
like germs when he laughed
"She's a slut."

or the silence in me then that rose
       like smothering black smoke—

or Barry's brother Don who broke their old dad's leg
       because he did their sister—

or the fish Don caught and cleaned alive
       right before my eyes,
       its heart unable to stop itself
       under his probing switchblade—

or the too-large army surplus clothes Don always wore
       as if a faded jacket could make a man
       of any dropout during the draft—

the creek where as long as daylight held
       we'd re-enact Bismarcks and Titanics
       making drowning cries for plastic disasters,
       then lob bigger rocks—

or Silly Willy who'd hug and kiss us
       at any hockey goal, saying, "They do it on TV!"
       until we yelled in his face, "EWW! Don't be GAY!"

or Will's sister whose hippy boyfriend on the couch
       pushed her panties down in her unzipped cutoffs
       stroking her musky crotch,
       which I'd never seen, let alone smelled....

or the dust-cloud rug by the TV that I stumbled on, crashed in—

or Will's mom then just watching the evening news crying—

or her silver-framed Navy officer photo
     making her weep
     not because he was dead
     but because, "He's gay," Will confessed,
     "...and I think I am too, like my dad."

the rich kid Larry with well-groomed hair and perfect clothes
     whose mom reclining on the couch
     stroked my head like a cat's
     until, half-hypnotized in my hair,
     her eyes were wet with yearnings
     and she called me her beautiful doll—

I could've been anyone
     if only the cells of the self
     would've let me out,
     if only the war on
     TV continually
     would ever turn off,
     but the time would come
     just once in an eon
     when I could be
     ecstatic as any thing
     beyond its self,
     when I was
     each injury,
     every injuring word,
     all the injured,
     and each sun-struck wave
     of grass blown to bliss,
     each inhale of sky in
     every tremulous body
     losing itself inside an other's,
     all the hiding selves who seek.

Tropical

With an open Bible and a heart
like the Arenal Volcano,
the street preacher
was spewing his own fire
and brimstone into the plaza.
I couldn't tell you what chastisements
charred his lips, but I can tell you
that all around him in San José
couples dizzied each other
with public kisses,
their arms and legs looped
into doughy love knots.
What verses the preacher
had chosen for his sermon
I couldn't say,
but I can tell you
that the air was abloom
with diesel exhaust and tropical fruit.
A man was selling
the last lottery tickets
of the day.
¡Los últimos! ¡Los últimos!
he baritoned,
and beside him in a smaller voice
a beggar begged.
As for the lone
young men that night,
many I saw; their eyes
hot and dark
as banked coals.
I couldn't tell you
which of them would

find a woman
or having found her
stick to her and love her
more or less
through the mountainous
years, but I can tell you
that everywhere dark Ticos and blond Ticos,
of citizens a veritable host,
were eating ice cream
that Sunday evening:
soft serve mostly,
but the scooped kind also.
¡Vainilla! ¡Chocolate!
crooned the vendors
from their carts and shops.
The people flocked about them,
on their tongues received
the cold and delicious blessings.
I can't tell you the name of the street
we strolled or why, holding hands, we felt
far from what troubled us,
but I can tell you
that the night was mild.
And it forgave much.

A Heart Caught Out

How articulate clouds
are when dammed
up dark bursts

like a heart
caught out
in the bumptious

spark and rattapallax
of rage—nothing
unlooses more

regrettable words,
nor more bitter
perfection

than the architecture
of drop or tear,
no more primordial

fear than the sky
falling from a mouth
you've kissed.

How like Echo
waiting for gravity
to have its way,

calling from caves,
where wet walls
weep stalactites

that ring the hollow
heart of longing
from our every word.

In Out of Night

The kerosene lantern
on the table excavates
the kitchen, singing
like a small waterfall.

The spangled windows weep,
as we dry, touching and speaking
softly, in the throbbing light.
In bed, we unpack all we need.

All night, rain makes
a drum of the house; our bodies
glow, bum, fade. All night,
the lantern on the table.

Coupled

The neck's crest bridges to the pricked ears.
The ears flick back when the neck rises.
I've read the loose-ring snaffle doubles
The hands' gestures to the horse's tongue:
Gloves mute their randomness, uncontrolled
Twitches of the fingers, blood's pulse.
I bought lilac nylon, suede-palmed to stick
To reins' leather slick with mare's sweat.
It lathers between her thighs on hot days,
Like today, as the video shows at home
In air-conditioning while I watch myself,
And her, working to learn. My technique's
Flaws bewilder us both: the ears flick back
When the neck rises. The back hollows,
The hocks drive out behind, the lumbosacral
Joint drops forward flexion, and the touch
Of my legs to her barrel offends, as the ears
Tell, and the neck, which, when correct,
Arches along the crest's length, the thick mane
Loose to the left, lifting in stride, bent
Like the tall grass through which a bull snake
Roiled, once, at the mare's feet, escaping
The wellhouse shade where last spring it shed
Skin. Neither of us flinched. We're bold
From weeks of training's concentration,
So I think back years, to lessons, horse shows,
Abandoned hopes, my belief I lacked
The talent, and know, now, decades late,
It was all wrong, including evaluation
Of error, and my life on top of bad riding

And worse guessing: I can't say I should've
Known but could've, since now, middle-aged,
Daily saddling the mare bought cheap
To relive old passions, ambitions, in secret
Dreams, I have gone on—gone and done it.
Sometimes, right. Her stiff side: right,
Meaning she is loath to stretch her left
But will, urged, considered, across the mowed
Bermuda pasture, mosquitoes choiring to feed,
Wood bees' stumbling feints, red dust, red mud,
Shoulder-in, leg yield, half-pass, rudiments
Of flying change, and my nights reading
And staring myself to sleep with remote control,
Slow mo, stop action, checking suspension
At the trot, why does she flirt her jaw, why fling
White lather, is the neck soft, or stiff, and which
Is wrong? Which goes round? Do I dare claim
We've done it right? Now that winning doesn't
Matter except alone, solitary ethic of pace,
Straddle, and afternoon light? I claim it
By the moment, where it lives. One night I read,
I must feel where each leg steps, not looking,
And next day did. Cantering, slow, hooves
Clocking spokes of a wheel. One night I read,
When you think you should take, give. Next
Day did: poured from suede palm, shoulder,
Sunburned, curled fingers, elbow's rusty hinge,
And the neck, chestnut, wet with honest rain,
Bowed to the bit, seeking touch through slight
Tension, chewing down air to meet metal
I could hold before her, floating: I won't betray
My joy when, between my calves, sides swelled,
And beneath my seat, back bounded like a doe,
Or ocean's wave, or love, of self, of rightness,

Balance, motion, everything. I'd say the world
Should've been there when I promised her that
Inch of space I'd plundered years and in obliging
Heart she returned the favor and gifted
Like a spring from earth's center: I'd say it
But the world was there, stretching snakeskin,
Bridging mare's footfalls everywhere, me
Mounted midst black-eyed susans, Indian
Paintbrush, one horsepower, dirt road west
Where pickups blurred, speeding, oblivious, wrong
As I'd been minutes before, and overhead both
Hawk and great blue heron, united in sky,
Gazing down, away, sailing like the sun
On high, and in my hands the clink of snaffle
Speaking back, soft, now, tongue, metal, forge
The rest of our lives worthwhile, soft, now, coupled.

The Sauce

Red plump globes just picked, halved in oil and salt to roast long and slow. Then pressed through the mill and—no skin or seed—just flesh and juice, like sweet soil, damp, and full of sun—

Or minced root and stem in the pan, sweet with time and heat. The wine, the broth—strained three times, from the shells of claws. Made less and less, like late sun eked thin on the long flank of earth—not quite gone—pink and gold and full of salt, and not much else—

Or leaves torn to strips, with oil and salt, plump seed, gored bulb. Crushed so it all bleeds green, like bits of shell left in the tide, like a storm, like its smell, like the slick and foam-pocked skin of the sea—

It should be just taste. There should not be too much. Fork and bread, tongue and salt. It should fill your dreams, and raise the sea. It should be enough.

Climbing the Tower
by Du Fu (712–770 C.E.)

Flowers by the high tower hurt the visitor's heart;

troubles are everywhere as I climb up to look down.

Spring colors along Brocade River bring heaven to earth;

floating clouds on Jade-fort Mountain blend then and now.

The court, like the North Star, in the end remained fixed;

may the Tibetans, west in the mountains, cease their raiding.

Even the pathetic Second Ruler still has his temple;

at the end of this day I will make a Liang-fu song.°

[764]

° *Liang-fu* is a small mountain; the *Liang-fu* song is a sad folksong often sung by *Zhu-ge Liang,* the minister who kept the government functioning during the reign of the incompetent Second Ruler of Shu. The Tower of the title was in *Cheng-du.*

Meeting Li Gui-Nian° in the South
by Du Fu (712–770 C.E.)

At the home of the Prince of *Qi*
    I have often seen you,
and in the hall of *Cui Jiu,*
    I have heard you sing.

Truly these southlands
    boast unrivalled scenery—
to see you once again
    when the flowers are falling.

[770]

° *Li Gui-nian* was an extraordinarily fine singer; favored by Emperor Xuan-zong, in whose court he often performed, he became not only famous but wealthy.

Mr. Mann Turns His Private House into a Hog Confinement Operation

The neighbors were at me night and day,
their caterwauling like insane cats in heat,

and so the grunting voices of my pigs
became a soft music. I loved their backs

at once sleek and bristled and their clear
preference for mud. I let them breed

promiscuously and they ran riot over
the whole place. I stopped closing doors.

I left windows open because of the smell
and ended up sleeping in the barn loft

among hay still green from the summer.
My imagination became the prodigal son.

They came for me twice, but I hid deep
in the woods behind the house piling leaves

across my body. I have never been
tempted to kiss any of the snouts

parading at my windows, nor to steal
any of the children hanging on the gate.

Putting Together a Bookshelf
with Albert Goldbarth

Al is up to his neck in red wine and I am trying like hell to follow
the instructions. He's going on and on about furniture as a comma
in the sentence we call home, there's crap everywhere, and I'm ready
to knock this guy flat on his ass if he doesn't shut up about the history
of the Burgundy Canal and how it would not have been finished
if it wasn't for a loan of 25 million francs, or how it's best to rinse
grapes under a faucet and wrap them in a paper towel to absorb any
excess water. He's got a connection for everything—a paint brush as
the hand of God and a can of paint as evidence that heaven is trying
to cover up the mistakes—I mean, this guy just doesn't know when to
stop. Now is not a good time to talk about the French. I am
      surrounded
by wood, it's getting late, and he's started on support groups and words
that go with them, that what I am dealing with is an alcoholic's strand
of DNA: fitting each screw in its right hole with the intent of having it
stand straight and bear the weight of the world. I don't have all night.

After the Star Party

Mount Wilson Observatory

The dome glows in the pines like a fallen moon,
announcing the last phase—
already I've stopped spinning
dim satellites or predictable cycles.
Guess it's some kind of release,
being away, being here with the
middle of the night's nebulous spirit,
this narrow ridge of tranquility
so far from home that troubles seem smaller,
as if distance were the answer.

Not much in the guest room
where I try to sleep: futon and table,
a mobile of sandalwood cranes
tipping their wings in scented air.
Bare walls, a floor so polished
even in the dark it reflects,
2 a.m. shadows spiraled in oak.
I wish my life were as simple as this room,
the mind made large and comfortable
by a few, wise choices.

Outside, a white gravel crescent leads
to the hundred inch where a star party
ended in a wet ring of cocktails—
glitter and idle talk plastered on metal walls,
the universe toasted as something to own.
Daily orbits dwarfed by Jupiter's
vast descent, the celestial loom's weave
of fire and air that has nothing to do with
what I hold onto—it's all temporary anyway,

a kind of cluttered emptiness,
my own body mostly space,
another illusion conjured by atoms,
a stunning effect, like these cranes
turning in their token piece of sky.
I keep getting it backwards, always
falling for science over spirit,
matter over mind.

Celebrity

Why do we claim your celebrity,
coming only as it did with your winter
death? In February, after the memorial service
though not the burial, which won't come until
spring when the ground's warm as milk or epidermis
we clot outside the church, form groves
against the wind, and pass your name around
like a plate. Mrs. Des Rochers—the obligatory
blue-haired lady with the spot on her head in the shape of Elvis
Costello or Jesus—wants us to believe she's been crying
but we all know better, the shared wisdom of the town
and of the winter moving through us like a charge,
like we had all joined hands to make a chain
and the one on each end would reach
to the electric mouth of the hand dryer
shiny in the men's bathroom on the first floor
of the old Houghton High School building
that's now a cluttered ruin. You'd huck your voice
around in class like you would a hoop
and get us all to move with you
to the bathroom, no spit-dirty chickens now
to put our mettle to your test. How
if we all held hands, that lusty electric mix
would assure and course right through us
like you coursed through the ice
and down through the lake
until you reflected off the bottom
in your one great flash bulb
terror of a moment
and maybe we would see your face
scouring the bottom of the ice
like curlers with their brushes do

or cartoonish talk show guests, elbowing
the inside curve of the television screen
and when one of us broke the electric link,
we'd all feel the jolt that was, I thought, like birth
or death, a shock and something new.

My Armless Brother's Armbone Soup
Tastes Like Love, Reflected

like salt
or footsteps in cement,
like cans of paint or guilt
rusted in the shed, like mint

and abstinence, sap fresh-bled from trees,
bacitracin smeared along the cut
for its antiseptic qualities
or simply put

direct upon the heart,
which, when caught in certain lights,
combusts and flies apart,
like rhubarb, or the night's

remains; like bear traps rusted open long,
like song

      *

like song
remains, like bear traps rusted open long,

like rhubarb, or nights
combusted, flown apart,
which, when caught in certain lights,
direct upon the heart

(or simply put
for its antiseptic qualities)
bacitracin smeared along the cut,
and abstinence like sap fresh-bled from trees,

rusted in the shed, like mint
like cans of paint or guilt
or footsteps in cement,
like salt

Rushmore

In memory of the activist, Anna Mae Aquash

They mask what they overlook, the bluffs
Around them, the reservations, Wounded Knee,
Legacy's raw and obdurate terrain.
Once there was a woman; not far, 1970s.
Ninety miles and a nation away,
An early spring unveiled her, hard as sculpture,
Slain under months of snow.
                                        Now they've exhumed
Her case, still shaping the truth. Well, it's simple:
There are no human shrines. She drank herself out
Of a smashed marriage, gave breath to songs, some shrill
As Dakota wind, smuggled food through a standoff
With marshals, had a way with children, especially
Her own.
                        One might contrast her unfinished work
With that of Gutzon Borglum, worshipful son
Of immigrants, who slowly carved while strung
From a bosun's seat, defaced Red Cloud's Black Hills
Then at the dedication confessed the land
As stolen. He never rendered the "wild and carefree"
Natives, though he yearned to.
                                                Some will say who
Knew about the bullet in her head. Some will say
Almost anything, like the FBI whispering
Threats in one ear, bribes in the other,
Who may have used her as an informer
Or hinted that they did.
                                        She wasn't Cary Grant's
Impeccable blond, the government spy
He saves in *North by Northwest,* dangling
From the monument while a subversive goon grinds

His hand with a shoe. It was Nixon stepping
On everyone's rights, obsessed with sympathizers,
A cinch to badmouth. But what of Lincoln,
She'd have asked, sad bass of the quartet, the one
With a conscience deep in the monolith, hanging
38 Sioux in Mankato because the settlers whooped
For hundreds, his moonlit cheek a sheer drop?

Maybe one day a repentant artist
Will idolize Leonard Peltier with granite
In the shadow prison a Bad Lands ridge of pines
Projects at dusk, Russell Means storming Rushmore.
But with Anna, he'll never have a chance.
How does one capture her smile, her daughters
So terribly young? Some people you can't make
Out of stone. Once they're gone, they're gone.

a field guide to the wild flowers of the moon

this spiky inflorescence
on the answer-phone
troubles the heart

the students are asked
which is the more stressful?
the bad news you anticipate
or the bad news that comes
when you least expect it?

and rats as usual
provide the answer

they droop like
stringy chrysanthemums
the colour of rust

their ulcers bloom brightly
like twitching anemones

they stumble through
falling petals of cancer

and those who have least
knowledge stumble first

towards the wall
towards the door
towards the window

through which
a sharp white
sickle moon
floats in a black sky
in its pale light
letters are lilac
enough to read

the future is round
and dark enough to see

Cancer in the Year of the Boar

for Sophie

When you were an hour in this world, breathing, I almost fainted
as I watched you through the glass. Daughter of my sister, welcome

to America, to this family of women who gather and save, who stash grocery bags
between major appliances and forget to reuse them. Your grandmother

used to hand me earthworms from her garden, even after they'd been chopped
with the shovel. I loved their dirt smell and the feel of them, wriggling in my palm,

and she says they grow back, heads or tails, whichever is missing. You should know
about her, how she digs giblets from a turkey with intent hands, and how we all

drive and talk, miss the turn and miles later, can't believe we've done it again.
Welcome, child, to the end of this century where you are no rebel against your country,

no number counted against us. You are not some lucky sequined dragon
delivered to save us, just your own brand-new heart, beating now

on its own. Someday, you and I will climb from this city to watch stars. See your sign
there like a cupped hand, a crab edging toward the moon. Look it up—

it means growth, cells multiplying, sprouting like tulip bulbs in our yards.
The difference is in the context of the word, the line-up of the planets

at the moment you turn the page. Within your great-grandmother's bones—
her liver or her used breasts- in your backyard, something sprouts. Mow it

or hack away at it, water it, decide to look away. Say what you want to, breathe the air
you've got, and drive fast like you know where you're going.

Last Spring

When we lost you
we asked winter to hold
its white sky, willed buds
to stay, for god's sake, closed
just a little longer. Spring
was a blind, senseless green,
a dark root, rude and rising.
We stared like sleepwalkers,
left your bike propped
by the back door where you
had left it, your thermostat to 67
with your prints still on the dial.
We dreamed ourselves back
to our December flannel beds
where we woke without pain.
Today I imagine you
in your purple duct-taped ski pants
and torn sweatshirt, tanned and
laughing, watching your dad
as he ties leather and horsehair
to the tree where he keeps you.
You must enter his heart now like
fire, coals smoldering or sudden blue
flames, here where spring
comes again like a swan
gliding on bitter water, her legs
kicking hard underneath.

The Cave

This cave is dark enough.
Even by night animals
run outlined in red.
Boars, bulls and bison.
A candle flickers the hunt.

A waiter with a white bib
yawns a welcome.

I see your tongue,
a host inviting.

Circus Days

Aunt Mary and my big
cousin Mary B bring me
to the circus.

Girls juggle and climb
the trapeze.

A man in a high hard hat
cracks a whip.
The elephants stand on drums.

The lion is sad.
His coat is patchy.
One and sixpence per child.

Later, at the Stella
I sit in the windowseat
with my Aunt Mary.

People pass but I see
only mangy lions
dragging sad tails.

Summer

By morning the wind will have erased our prints. The polite gathering
of sand, you say, a carpet cleaner bored for the evening, bored of our
mess. The breath of brackish water

through my window. Every Sunday you bring down the drapes and
shake clean the salt. The bay outside remembers my smell. Hours after
I leave, it remembers to float through my hands;

the marred accent of the wave, thick in consistency. Though I try, I
am seven this summer and too wild to be my mother's ballerina. After
the recital, I use the leotard, gold and sky-blue,

as a flag for a sandcastle. The crown still on my head, I ask you,
carefully, to remove the pins from the bun. I am walking toward the
tide, washing through the swell,

the fold against my step. Filling a red bucket with water, slowly trying
the boundaries maintained by your voice. I am prepared to flood my
own standing village: Buildings

shaped with abandoned jars and cadence. I line the walls with seaweed
and molded lace. The water rushes through caves wide as my fist and
canals turn to swamps.

I am not kind, not enough to save the swarming creatures, marinating
in their flooded home. You hold the plastic shovel in your teeth,
watch the persistent and gentle destruction. My feet burrow into the
peppered sand. I am planted.

stupid

ma sayed when i got kicked in the head by the horse i turned stupid but pa sayed it ain't so i were stupid long fore that   either way i know i'm stupid cause everybody keep telling me   teachers in school back when i went to school teld me   pastor sheridan he teld me   doctor sherry marchalongus told me   she sayed that's why i killed jenny jane

i didn't know i killed jenny jane   but doctor sherry she the doctor and she say i the one who done it   she must know cause she is smarter than me   everybodys smarter than me

what happened is this   jenny jane she not so smart neither and she were never kicked in the head   back in school when we were each 10 year old we were put in class together class for stupid kids me and jenny jane been friends 20 years

jenny jane she kind of pretty with a nose like the thimble ma put on her finger when she sewed when she still alive   jenny jane always kind of shy and she liked to smile and she sayed she smile most when she with me but i know other boys liked her and that how she got in trouble them two times   so sometimes she go with them and they did things with her she would not let me do with her until after she have two babies and mister and missus jamisen made her go to the hospital up in pocatello so she would not have no more babies since she could never remember to take them pills and after social services come and took her babies away jenny jane she cried so hard when they got taken and she did not smile for a real long time and one day she sayed if any of them boys who made her with babies sayed they would marry her she thinks social services would of let her keep her babies but them boys would not say that   one of them jeff told her she too stupid to marry and that did not bother her cause just like me she become use to people saying that but then he sayed she too ugly to marry and that made her cry real bad cause only nice thing anybody ever sayed to her is she is pretty and her mama and her papa and me we all told her that a hundred thousand times but jeff saying she ugly made her not believe the hundred thousand million times we told her so i told jeff he mean and he told me a bad thing   to have sex with myself   so i told him again and i hit him with my palm right across his face and i know i hurt him and he just look at me with his mouth open and his eyes real wide and he look the stupid one then

anyway jenny jane and me we walking along the canal holding hands even though i am now 37 years old and jenny jane is 37 years old too and it a real hot day and jenny jane says she real thirsty and i tell jenny jane she can not drink the canal water and she sayed silly i know that and she smile like she like me and she told me she ain't been with no boy or man in a real long time and i says i am a boy or man and i were with her and she sayed silly and i sayed you mean like doing stuff together and we lay down there in the field on the edge of the alphalpha that's one of my favorite words alphalpha and a long time ago i asked pa to help me spel it and he did and i practiced all one night and i learnt to spel it by heart and i ain't never speld it wrong since and sometimes i just say to people do you know how to spel alphalpha and they look at me and i spel it right there and joey hamilton he one time sayed i speld it wrong but i know i didn't so i hit him and later the sherriff man come to my home and tell my pa i can't go hitting people and if i do they will put me in the state home upstate and pa sayed he would make real certain i didn't hit no body no more and so i never hit no body no more except 3 times i hit them boys who were all from out of town and they did not know who i was and they sayed something bad about jenny jane they sayed she had a fat behind and i told them not to say that and to make sure they did not i hit all three of them with my hand rolled up not my palm and i hurt two of them real bad one with a bloody eye the other with some teeth on the ground and the third told them two to leave with him and jenny jane thanked me for defending her honor and that was the first time we layed down together and that was a real long time ago

well this one time we layed down near the canal there were lots of flys and while she is under me instead of putting her hands on my back or my behind like she usually done she kept waving her hands to keep them flys away and she kept saying go way go way go way and

just then mister slaughter come along shouting something at us   i
first do not pay no attention cause i am thinking about them flys and
also i am thinking about me and jenny jane laying down together and
then i do hear what mister slaughter is yelling   he is yelling get off
jenny jane and at first i think that is dumb because one time i saw his
sheep doing the same thing when i was standing right next to him
and he just sayed it were funny to watch and it made him feel like a
voyager   but this time he were not laughing and he screaming and
jenny jane she kept waving at them flys and yelling for them to go way
and before i know just where mister slaughter is his body hits into my
body and i were on the ground with mister slaughter on top a me and
he got to his feet and he stood over me and he sayed i must not make
jenny jane do nothing she do not want to do and jenny jane sayed it
were all right cause she wanted to but mister slaughter did not hear
her i guess and he told me he were going to have to call the sherriff
man and he made us walk with him to his house   he sayed to me i
know you ain't real smart and that most of the time you are a good
person but it is wrong to make a girl do things she do not want to do
and jenny jane sayed she did want to do it and mister slaughter sayed
he could tell by the way she were waving and swinging and screaming
that were not the truth and he knew she were not real smart neither
and he were just helping her to understand that even though she not
real smart she did not have to let no body force her to do things and
after a time mister slaughter's wife come in and guv us milk and apple
pie   the sherriff man come and mister slaughter talk to him and then
he talk to us and he wrote down things and he told us we had to come
with him and he made me sit in the back of his sherriff automobile
and told jenny jane to sit in the front and there was a cage between
us and i put my fingers through it and jenny jane she put her fingers
through it and we held hands best we could and we stared at each
other and the sherriff man he took us to jenny jane's place and we
all got out and the sherriff man he spoke to jenny jane's mama cause
her papa he died four years ago and her mama took jenny jane to the
side a the shed and they talked for a real long time and then missus
jamisen come back and she told the sherriff man i ain't gonna put no

179

charges on larry here that's my name larry lawrence   the sherriff man sayed you certain missus jamisen and missus jamisen sayed she were that she were real sure jenny jane were just telling them flys go way and ever since jenny jane went to the hospital her ma and pa believed there were not much times for jenny jane to enjoy life and she were after all a woman and that she and mister jamisen always liked me caused no one else had so much in common with jenny jane and they knew i would never ever hurt her and the sherriff man said he had to take into consideration what mister slaughter teld him and then he spoke to jenny jane and then he told me get in the sherriff automobile and when i started to get in the back seat he sayed no lawrence get in the front seat and i did and he drove me to the place where i live   it were kind of up in the mountains after you drive a real long time on a dirt road and the sherriff man asked if i would be all right and i sayed yes why not and he sayed because your ma and pa are dead and you live alone and everybody knows you can not take care of yourself but i teld him i could and i told him about the check i get every month from the state and he sayed he knew about that and he told me he been thinking i got to be real careful cause i did not have the ability to tell people what i were really doing sometime and poor jenny jane that's what he called her poor jenny jane couldn't help me out in that neither and i sayed something i didn't want to say but it just come out i sayed i know people don't always understand me cause i am stupid and he sayed ain't never been a truer thing sayed

i stayed home two days after the sherriff man took me there then jenny jane come over and talk to me and we decided to walk down to the cracker barrell which is the only store in franklin and where i get my food and we held hands walking down the long dirt road and then the narrow paved road and a pickup truck with some teenage boys on the back go by and two of the boys yelled at us about being stupid and one of them yelling we were too stupid to know how to do it but he didn't say what it were we were too stupid to know how to do and that's when i sayed to jenny jane i ain't too stupid to love you and she sayed she weren't too stupid to love me too and even though we did things together for 20 years or more that that were the first time i told her i loved her and it were the first time she told me she loved me and i felt real good about that about as good as i ever felt about anything

   i felt so good i wanted to give her a gift so when we got to the cracker barrell i look at the stuff they had and mostly they had cans of food and boxes of food but they sold some t-shirts and one of them were real pretty and it had a picture of mountains and it sayed idaho and i took it off the hanger and held it up next to jenny jane and it looked real good and i asked her to put it on and she were real happy and we took two ice cream sandwiches from the freezer and payed for them ice cream sandwiches   we payed the girl behind the counter and there were another girl who worked there and she were putting cans and stuff on shelves   we went outside and the girl putting stuff on the shelf she sayed something but i weren't paying no mind and me and jenny jane sat on the steps of the porch and ate our ice cream sandwiches and that's when the girl come out behind us and she sayed in a real angry voice i told you two stupids to put the t-shirt back and jenny jane looked real hurt and i sayed it's jenny jane's i give it to her as a present and the girl sayed if you don't put the t-shirt back i am going to call the sherriff man and have you arrested and i sayed we don't have to give it back and just then i remembered i had not payed for the t-shirt but the girl she went inside so i went in after her and i took money from my pocket and sayed i would pay for the shirt and jenny jane she come in after me and the girl who called us stupids were on the telephone but the other girl she took my money   me and jenny jane we left the store and we started to walk to my home and jenny jane were saying to me we didn't do nothing wrong and just then the girl who had been on the telephone come out and run up to us and grabbed jenny jane and sayed you wait here you stupid something but i had both her hands on jenny jane's arm and pulled real hard and i could tell she were hurting jenny jane and scaring her and i sayed let jenny jane alone but the girl didn't pay me no mind and i hit on her arms to let jenny jane go and when she didn't i hit her again this time harder and she fell on the ground and started saying bad words about me and calling me stupid and these bad words that ma and pa taught

me never to never say and jenny jane asked her if she were all right
if she needed help and jenny jane she bent over to try to help the girl
and the girl just punched jenny jane right in the mouth real hard and
blood come and i wanted to hit that girl again but i didn't and i took
jenny jane by the hand and i ran and she had to run with me and our
ice cream sandwiches were melting and jenny jane were crying and i
could tell she were real scared

the next day is when i met doctor sherry   the sherriff man
come to my house and sayed i had to go with him   i tried to explain
i did pay for the t-shirt and he sayed it didn't matter none and he
made me get in his sherriff automobile and he took me to a place that
weren't exactly like a hospital but they put me in a room and doctor
sherry come in and she talk to me a long time and made me take
some tests with real hard questions   She were not a nice person   i
sayed i want to go home and she sayed shut up   i sayed i want to see
if jenny jane is all right and she sayed shut up   i sayed i did not like
having to answer questions and she sayed shut up

she left the room and a man come and took me to a room that
had a bed and a plastic chair and nothing else except a picture on the
wall   the picture had a cow and i looked at the picture and i cried
he put me in it and he left and locked the door

i did not see nobody for two days except for the man who
brought me eggs and sausage in the morning and a peanut butter
sandwich for lunch and chicken legs for dinner both days the same
food and when i told him i would like an orange he sayed i will see
what i can do and later he brought me an orange and he sayed do not
tell missus hitler i give you this

jenny jane come to see me the next day   her mama sat behind
jenny jane and jenny jane and i sat on different sides of a table and
we were told we could not touch and i told jenny jane i loved her and
jenny jane told me she loved me and she sayed she would come to see
me everyday and her mama leaned up to her and sayed there were a
rule against that and she could come only once a week and jenny jane
sayed she would write every day or ask her mama to write since she
did not write so good and i sayed i knew how to write i love you and

would write that and she smiled real pretty

i wrote to jenny jane that night and every day and i never did not write and every letter i wrote i sayed i love you

my first letter from jenny jane come 2 days later and the envelop it were open and when i took out the letter i saw thick black marks on it   some thick black lines had been drawn over some words so i could not read them   two or three words just above where jenny jane signed her name were covered in black and i knew that were where jenny jane wrote she love me and i felt real good she wrote it and real sad somebody done put a black mark on it

some days later doctor sherry come in and hand me a letter and she sayed she need to read them first and that was why some words were with black on them and she sayed i too stupid to read some things and stupid people should not fool themselves to believe things were true that were not true

i sayed to doctor sherry why do you hate me   it were something i were thinking about many days to say to her and when i sayed it she look real mean with her eyes close to each other and she sayed in a real low voice so i had to listen real hard to hear i do not hate you i know all about your kind and then she give me another test and she sayed the reason she give me the new test were to prove one more time i am stupid but this time it were also to prove i were dangerous to people   the test were to pick up some blocks she put on the floor and throw them against the wall and she asked me if i were too stupid to do that and she had one of them cameras that take pictures to show on television and when i threw the blocks against the wall she told me to throw them hard and to yell when i did and to pretend i were very angry and i did cause she were telling me to do them things

later that day a man from the state come in and his name were seth and he teld me tomorrow i would go to see a judge and i sayed did the sherriff man say i did not pay for the t-shirt and i sayed i did pay and he sayed no that were all in the passed and the judge would meet me in his office not in the court and he would come cause the state did not provide lawyers in cases like mine but he would do the best he could to look out for me and the only other person there would be doctor Sherry and he knew she would say i were dangerous to people and i need to be locked up forever and he sayed he know that were not true and he hoped he could tell the judge that and i asked him could jenny jane come and he sayed no he were sorry and i sayed could jenny jane come to see me first and he sayed he could arrange that

real early next morning jenny jane and her mama come to see me and jenny jane she tell me she love me and why did i not write to her and i sayed i did and she sayed not one letter come to her home and she turn to her mama and sayed mama did any letters come from lawrence and her mama sayed no and that she were sorry and i told her i wrote every day and that in every letter i wrote down i love you then the man in the uniform come over and he sayed to me real quiet so jenny jane could not hear missus hitler sayed the visit could be only 5 minutes but if i wanted to i could go over to jenny jane and be with her so i went around the table and i asked jenny jane if i could hold her and she put her arms around me and she kissed me and i kissed her and i told her i loved her and she told me she loved me and then the guard sayed he were sorry and then i sayed goodbye jenny jane and jenny jane she sayed goodbye lawrence

seth sat in the back of the automobile with me when we drove to see the judge and doctor sherry sat up front with the driver who were a guard in a blue uniform

the judge did not look like a judge cause he did not have on no black dress   he wore a suit that were gray and he smiled like he were friendly

doctor sherry sayed i dangerous i attack many people and she showed the judge papers she sayed sherriff men wrote out and that they went back to when i was very young and still in school for stupid children and then she showed the judge something on television and it were me throwing blocks only no body could hear doctor sherry tell me throw them and every body could see me screaming but nobody could hear me screaming and doctor sherry sayed what were on the television proved i should be locked away and then she sayed real slow stupidity is dangerous to society i started to say something but seth he touched my arm and i knowed he did not want me to talk   what i wanted to say is she told me to throw them blocks and i wanted to ask her why she hated me but seth he spoke and he sayed to the judge

doctor sherry always want to lock up people like me and he sayed it were not the right thing to do and i could see doctor sherry were very angry with seth and then she sayed she were the leading special person in all of idaho in the area of stupidity and she had wrote three books about it and she had committed her whole life to the problem of stupid people

the judge put up his hand and doctor sherry stopped speaking and the judge sayed he knew she were admired by other people who knew things too but he wanted to consider the pattern of things she sayed and he sayed she were always saying people like me should be locked up and he were wondering why she never not one single time ever sayed somebody should not be locked up

doctor sherry sayed it were because people like me were dangerous

the judge sayed he would think about it and then he asked me if i understood what everybody were saying and i sayed i think i did and i sayed i never hurt nobody on purpose and i told him about them boys who sayed a bad thing about jenny jane and how i told them not to and he sayed maybe i did the right thing but he would have to think about that too

seth and doctor sherry and the guard and me we drove back to the place where they test stupid people   that night i did not sleep cause i were thinking so much about maybe never ever being able to see jenny jane but i did not cry

the next day jenny jane come to see me but her mama were not with her and jenny jane sayed a car come to drive her and the man in it sayed her mother could not come and that doctor sherry told the man to tell her she were going to see me and her mama thought about it real hard but sayed it were all right   then the guard told me and jenny jane to go to my room and we sat in there and we held hands and jenny jane sayed if they put me in a place where no body could

185

come see me she would do something to make them put her in the same place   she sayed if she could not do that she would learn to use dynamite and blow up the wall and i could come out and we could run away together   she sayed she loved me so much   i sayed i loved her so much

then doctor sherry come in and she sayed jenny jane stay and she tell me go down the hall to where the television were and she and jenny jane would talk and i were not to come back into my room until she come to get me and if i come back before that it would be real bad and i would be locked away for sure and were i too stupid to understand that and i sayed i understand that and i went out and i went to the television room and other men and some women were there and they were watching something on the television and they were laughing but i do not know what they were watching cause i could not pay no attention thinking bout jenny jane and what doctor sherry and her were talking about and there were another show on the televison and another and i wanted to go back to the room and see jenny jane but i daren't cause of what doctor sherry sayed she would do and i knowed she would tell the judge i did not do what she told me to do and maybe the judge might say cause of that i had to be locked away   i do not know how judges think

then doctor sherry she come into the room and she told me go to your room and when i go doctor sherry she lock the door behind me and i sayed where is jenny jane but doctor sherry just walk away and i watched her through the little window in the door with its real thick glass and then i sat on my bed and then i do not know why but i thought something is wrong so i got up and i looked around and i got down on my knees and i see jenny jane under the bed and i sayed jenny jane what is wrong and she don't say nothing and i touch her and push her shoulder and say jenny jane jenny jane jenny jane and she still do not say nothing and then i put my hand on her hand and it seem funny maybe cause it the first time i ever touch her hand she did not touch my hand back so i put my hand on her arm and i pull a little and i know i were crying and i pulled a little more and a little harder and i pulled her out and her eyes are open and she is looking at nothing and i kiss her and i say jenny jane jenny jane jenny jane

now i am in the place they put stupid people who are dangerous
to people who are not stupid and once jenny jane's mama come to
see me and she sayed she is not angry with me for what i done and
i know she mean she think i the one who killed jenny jane and i am
not sure if i am or not   at first i thought for sure i were not but then
doctor sherry sayed the reason i did not know i were the one is cause
i am too stupid and a sherriff man sayed i done it cause i the one in
the room when jenny jane were found by the guard and when i sayed
i were watching television the sherriff man sayed there were lots of
time i were not watching and seth sayed what happened were terrible
and he knew i did not really mean to hurt jenny jane but i must have
held her so much i hurt her real bad and he sayed sometimes you
hurt people by holding them real hard and you do not know you are
holding them real hard

the only other person who come to see me were doctor sherry
and she sayed i were too stupid to know i killed jenny jane and i were
too stupid for the judge to want to see me and i were too stupid to
know what the truth were the last thing doctor sherry ever sayed to
me were something she sayed when i sayed maybe you hurt jenny jane
and she sayed do you think i am the stupid one do you think i am the
one who is a danger to people and i did not know what to say cause i
know she ain't stupid like me so i did not say nothing

i almost never say nothing no more except when i am alone in
the room with iron bars on the window and two steps from one side
to the other and four steps from one end to the other and the door
is made of metal and it does not have a window and other persons in
other rooms near mine make noises like dogs singing all day long and
all night long and the only noise i make is to say jenny jane jenny jane
jenny jane jenny jane jenny jane jenny jane jenny jane

No Cause for Alarm

Last night, while backing his Cherokee into the garage, Tom Boyd spotted his neighbor, Dr. Gallant, standing in a bright upstairs window of his house. He was quietly standing, his gaze moving somewhere past Tom's roof, probably far down Indian Hill at Worchester and all its lights. Not long before, Tom had seen Mrs. Gallant lugging a suitcase in each hand down their long, steep driveway and zoom away in a black sports car. Now, mowing grass with the new Lawn King he had charged on his and his wife's first credit card together, Tom couldn't get Mrs. Gallant out of his head. Every time he turned to start another row, he still saw her straw hat coming down the driveway.

Tom inhaled deeply. He loved the smell of freshly cut grass, and considered it to be an unforeseen but very welcome perk of home ownership. This weekend, he planned to catch up on his yard work because the Family Vision Center he managed was closed for renovations. As he strolled along, staining the toes of his sneakers green, enjoying the vibration in his palms and admiring the Lawn King, he fantasized about preparing dinner for Suzanne later tonight, wine and candles and all. Suzanne copyedited obituaries for the *Telegram & Gazette* and worked late every Saturday. He didn't know how to cook anything, though—just hotdogs, eggs, and grilled cheese.

Tom had finished half his front lawn and was moving closer to the Gallants' yard thinking about what Dr. Gallant could or couldn't cook, when the Lawn King sputtered twice and died. He checked the gas tank (it was empty), and the gas can in the garage (also empty). Next door, the Gallants' colonial stood quiet and peaceful on its small hill of deep grass. He could borrow some gas from Dr. Gallant, and maybe find out what had happened with his wife while he was at it. He had heard from another neighbor that Gallant was a history professor at Clark who spent all his time reading books—some kind of weirdo, the neighbor had said. Tom had only spoken to Dr. Gallant twice before. He had been friendly enough, if not exactly warm.

Halfway up the Gallants' driveway, Tom was startled by a loud crash from behind the house. He eased open the big wooden door of the stockade fence that enclosed the backyard. The first thing he noticed was a pool filled not with water but with a mountain of furniture—kitchen table and chairs, an upside-down filing cabinet spewing papers, a couch, a bookcase, books, curtains, curtain rods. There was much, much more.

Tom circled the shallow end, taking in the scattered kitchen utensils and broken plates, wondering whether coming here would be a big mistake. A coffee table lay on its back with a leg broken off, next to an exploded television set.

Something sailed into his peripheral vision, and he ducked as a dresser drawer smashed to pieces so near him that Tom felt the splinters stutter against his bare legs. He looked up.

Dr. Gallant was standing on the balcony overlooking the swimming pool. He was wearing a bathrobe, and a cigarette was sticking out of his down-turning mouth. He held a lighter to the cigarette, and his hand shook as he lit it, inhaled deeply. He wasn't wearing his glasses, Tom noticed, and the shadows under his eyes and his thick, disheveled gray hair made him look as though he hadn't slept in days. Even his walrus mustache was mussed.

Dr. Gallant exhaled a funnel of smoke that hung for a moment in the thick heat. "It all makes perfect sense," he said.

Tom motioned over his shoulder. "I was just cutting the grass...."

"Yes, Mr. Boyd. May I say the beauty of your home is surpassed only by that of your wife? And that Vision Center, I took your advice and bought a new pair of lenses for my reading glasses." He took his bifocals out of his pocket and donned them. "I see much better now."

"I just saw on the news where this guy in Maine had to drain his pool because he found a moose in it." Tom was making this up, but Dr. Gallant was nodding as though he had heard it too.

"I drowned in this pool the very first night we filled it. We made love right there—" He pointed to the shallow end, where a painting of a horse was impaled by a chair leg. "A bright night, full moon. Do you know what Cicero said, Mr. Boyd? 'Not to know what happened before one was born is always to be a child.'"

189

"I'm not sure—"

"They don't allow you to be sure! This is the third time she's left me. Don't be surprised at anything they do, Mr. Boyd." Gallant grabbed a piece of silk that had been draped over the railing. "So why can't I sleep with her nightgown strewn across the carpet, her dresser drawers sticking out like so many tongues? I can't sleep until I erase her." He pitched the balled-up cloth from the balcony. It unfurled into a nightgown and dropped onto the pile of furniture.

Tom rubbed the back of his neck. "I'd give you a hand, but I—"

"She mocks me," Dr. Gallant said, oblivious or unconcerned with Tom's growing discomfort. He pulled a piece of paper from his robe and shook it in his fist. "Such an elegant letter!" With his other hand, he flicked the cigarette, now only a smoldering stub, into a bush against the base of the house and then steadied himself against the railing.

A lawn mower hid under a piece of canvas a few feet from the bush. There was a large, red jerry can beside it, but Tom had already decided to get his gas elsewhere.

"I was like you once," Dr. Gallant said, still staring at the letter. "Mowing back and forth, back and forth, up and down. You give it all the attention in the world and what does it do? It just grows back. But then again, there's nothing like the smell of a freshly mown lawn, is there?" He closed his eyes, sniffed. "You should get yourself a swimming pool."

Tom nodded. He envisioned a pool, then a white-oak bed floating in it. "Things are kind of tight right now."

A smile stretched Dr. Gallant's lips. "Enjoy the tight times; you'll appreciate them when you're my age." He chuckled and started coughing. He still held the letter in front of his face, and used it now to wave Tom away.

After his visit with Dr. Gallant, Tom spent the afternoon in his recliner in the living room, thinking about his wife, thinking of earlier days when everything had been new. Once, they had made love in a row boat in the middle of Lake Quinsigamond, her squatting over him in her bare feet, him grasping the sides of the boat, and later, both of them singing, "Row row row your boat," as they headed to shore. He had thought then that life couldn't get better. He'd just spent most of the afternoon trying to convince himself he was wrong.

"Why didn't you ask him what happened, if you were so concerned?" Suzanne was asking now.

Tom stood naked in the doorway between the bedroom and bathroom, pulling a towel across his wet back. Suzanne sat on the white-oak bed before him, legs crossed, her foot bobbing so that her ankle bracelets tinkled.

"She left him. What more is there to ask?"

Suzanne kept at it with her foot. "Her side of things."

Tom realized that she had a new hairstyle. It looked like a mop. "Maybe he can't get it up any more." He hiked his ankle onto his knee and dried between the toes.

"I doubt that's it."

Tom didn't care for the way a piece of her hair hung down, covering one eye. She looked like somebody else. "I'll still love you when your hair is gray and you're fat."

"And I'll love you when the runways on the top of your head join in the back to form a ring." She laughed and had said this with so little forethought that it sounded rehearsed. She stood. "If I ever leave you, don't trash the house."

Tom watched the footsteps she made on the carpet slowly disappear behind her as she walked to the mirror. Sticking out from under the bed, her crumpled nightgown reminded Tom of something he wanted to say.

"Don't," she said, twisting her lipstick.

"They were married a long time. Decades."

She and her reflection bent toward each other and applied lipstick. Tom turned, went into the bathroom and stood before the mirror. When he lifted his razor, he saw her in the doorway behind him.

"Let's have a nice meal tonight, okay?"

Tom squirted a blob of shaving cream onto his palm and

191

watched her wrap her arms around the waist of the man in the mirror.

"No silly arguments," she continued.

"Okay, Zana-bean. But first, come with me next door. Make sure he's all right."

The sky above them was dark, the horizon frozen with pink swirls, as they moved across the grass toward the Gallants' house. There was smoke in the sky above the chimney. A loud crackling came from behind the house. Tom and Suzanne glanced at each other nervously. They pushed the tall wooden door open, and heat struck them as though they had stepped into a kiln. Huge orange and yellow flames licked at the bottom of the balcony, and skeins of black smoke twisted up into the night air. Flames reflected in the windows—the pool was ablaze.

Suzanne dashed past Tom toward the house, shielding her face with her arm and shouting over her shoulder, "Find a hose!" She yanked the sliding glass door open, and vanished inside.

Tom took a few steps toward the pool, but was stopped by the heat. He recognized the recliner propped in the middle of the blaze like an abandoned throne spitting flames. A partially melted toothbrush flamed on the tiles that ringed the pool, a puddle of burning pink plastic. He had a sudden vision of lying in bed, reading, while Mrs. Gallant brushed her teeth in her nightgown. He backed up a pace. A light breeze came from behind and blew across his arms and neck.

Tom entered the kitchen and found his wife standing amid broken glass. "I called the police," she said quietly. She was staring past him, her lips parted. The fire crackled outside, and all of the windows glowed.

They found Dr. Gallant in a lawn chair in the shadows of the living room, facing an empty fireplace and motionless, except for the lifting of a lit cigarette to his mouth. Smoke hung in the air above his head. He was wearing his bathrobe, his legs crossed and his feet on the hearth, exposing dark socks and a pair of wing-tips. The room was otherwise entirely bare but for a few nails on the walls.

Dr. Gallant turned then, expressionless. After a second, he returned his gaze to the fireplace. Tom waited for Suzanne to say something. This might be too much for her—a man lounging, smoking, after burning all that he owned, which included many things that she and Tom could not yet afford. She took a small step, and then they both inched into the room.

"Are you okay?" she asked him, her voice calm and soft.

Dr. Gallant raised the cigarette to his lips. The cherry glowed orange. Without turning, he said, "So nice to see you again, Mrs. Boyd."

Flames flickered in the window to Tom's left. "Why don't we wait outside?" he suggested.

Suzanne shot him an irritated look. "The firemen are on the way. Everything's fine."

"Mrs. Boyd," Dr. Gallant said, "your voice is very much like my wife's. The way it hides emotion behind a veil of civility. I beg your pardon, but it's true, isn't it?"

"Help is on the way," Suzanne repeated.

"Hell, Mrs. Boyd, is a vast and unbottom'd pit, a place paved with women's tongues."

Tom cringed. Suzanne wouldn't take this kind of talk for long.

Dr. Gallant blew a long stream of smoke. "A lake of fire and brimstone whose flames are unquenchable, and whose smoke ascendeth forever and ever." He smiled at the ceiling. "I first kissed her in her mother's driveway, 1956. Warm chocolate eyes. The first time she left me, I wept. She said then, and would say now, I imagine, that I read too much." Dr. Gallant inhaled, shook his head ruefully, and smoke leaked from his nostrils. "The life of a woman is full of woe—" He popped out of the recliner and held his hands out to Suzanne. His robe exposed a T-shirt and boxers. "One last dance before you go."

Suzanne smiled but did not take his hands, so Dr. Gallant dropped his cigarette on the floor and stepped on it. "Tom, Tom, Tom," he said. "May I call you Tom? She was not made out of his head, sir, to rule and govern the man, nor was she made out of his

193

feet, sir, by man to be trampled upon."

Tom didn't know what to do. Suzanne burst out laughing.

Dr. Gallant began to sing what sounded to Tom like opera. He sang deeply, holding his arms out in front of his body, chin raised, dancing with an imaginary partner, his wing-tips shuffling across the wooden floor toward Suzanne. She became his partner after all, slipping between his raised arms as though they had rehearsed. They floated to the corners of the room and back.

"Where the hell are the firemen?" Tom asked, although clearly no one was listening.

"I haven't been dancing since 1978, her sister's third wedding," Dr. Gallant said to Tom. "Everything comes in threes. I take it she's your first?"

"And last," Tom said.

"May she be just that," Dr. Gallant said, reaching for Suzanne's cheek. She let him touch it. "There is no worse evil than a bad woman." He caressed her with his thumb. "And nothing has ever been produced better than a good one." He slid his hand from her cheek, slowly, letting his fingertips linger under her chin.

Tom wanted Suzanne to let him have it this time. Instead, she blushed.

Without another word, Dr. Gallant released her and returned to the chair before the fireplace. He didn't move again.

When sirens filled the neighborhood, Tom said, "You go, honey. I'll stay with him."

Suzanne gave him a look, one of her sardonic smiles with her lips pressed together. "We'll both stay." She went to Dr. Gallant, who was whispering to himself.

Suzanne sat on the hearth, took his hand and held it on her lap.

"I knew about all her lovers, Tom. May I call you Tom?"

Just then the front door opened. Dr. Gallant jerked at the sound, a sudden look of panic on his face. A woman stood in the living room wearing a big dirty yellow coat and trousers, fluorescent orange striped across her chest, wrists and ankles. She tipped her fireman's hat back, her face deadpan.

"Whose house is this?" she asked.

Dr. Gallant eyed her suspiciously. "I believe it's mine."

"And you?" she asked Tom.

"We're friends," Suzanne said. "We live next door."

The woman nodded to Suzanne and identified herself as a Worchester City fire captain. She asked Dr. Gallant a lot of questions, all of which he handled with the utmost ease, speaking softly and always respectfully. She motioned to Suzanne and they moved across the room and whispered by a window facing the pool. Light played on their faces, and firemen shouted in the background.

"Wives like hats," Dr. Gallant said, nodding toward the women. "All kinds of hats. They wear them to be someone else."

Tom lay bare-chested on the bed with his hands locked behind his head. They had said only a few words over pizza at the kitchen table, because it was late and they were anxious to go to sleep. The fire captain had told them before they left that Dr. Gallant wasn't in any real trouble, though he would have to submit to a psychological evaluation.

"That was something else," Tom said at last. The bathroom door was ajar and in the sliver of mirror he watched his wife undress.

"Makes you wonder." She pulled her bra over her head and tossed it on the floor. "He didn't say anything else to you?"

"She left him a note."

"What did it say?" She moved and he couldn't see her anymore. The water was running.

"How would I know?"

She came out in her underwear and turned off the lights. She went to the dresser and opened a drawer in the dark. Her figure was barely discernible. When she slipped beneath the covers, she was wearing a sweatshirt. He bent his leg and bumped his knee against her. She had sweat pants on as well. It had been so long since they'd had sex, she didn't even try anymore.

"You cold?" he asked.

She replied only when Tom had let himself believe that she had

195

fallen asleep, and then, she answered an unspoken question. "I hate my job. It's like losing a little piece of myself every time I read that shit." In the dark, Tom turned to her but remained silent. "They're all the same, nobody stands out. Especially the women. Imagine living your whole life and all anybody can say about you is that you were a *homemaker*."

The telephone rang. Tom answered it.

"I wanted to apologize."

"No, Dr. Gallant, we're good. Don't worry."

"Splendid, splendid." Dr. Gallant's voice was strangely persistent. "All's well at this end. I wanted to thank you both for coming to me in my hour of need, shall we say."

"Not a problem," Tom said. Suzanne was listening.

"I called to invite you both over for dinner."

"Great," Tom said.

"I've a pot of soup on, my own recipe, though it's been a while since I've made it—twenty-three years to be precise—but there is plenty for all. It should be done within the hour."

Tom sat up. "Now?"

"Is it too late?"

"We're already in bed," Tom said.

"Bed," Dr. Gallant repeated. "Yes, well maybe some other time, then. I won't keep you from doing whatever it is that you were doing or were about to do."

He hung up, and Tom held the receiver for a moment, the dial tone roaring in his ears. The bedroom was still dark, but he could see shapes now. "Yes of course we will," he said into the dead phone. He paused. "She's right here, safe and sound. Yeah, I do, too. Good night to you, too." Tom hung up the phone.

Suzanne rolled over to face him. "What did he want?"

Tom told her about the soup. "And he wanted to know what we were doing in bed."

"Passion is a burning forehead and a parching tongue," Suzanne said.

"What is that supposed to mean?"

"That's what he said to me before we left."

The telephone rang again. It seemed louder this time. Tom let it ring.

Suzanne stretched across him. "Hello? Yes." She listened for a few seconds. "Sure, but only if you call me Suzanne." She paused, her elbow pressing painfully against Tom's thigh. "Yes, I love it like that. Good night."

Tom closed his eyes. He felt her shift, heard the receiver click against its cradle.

"You love what like what?" he asked after it became obvious she wasn't going to volunteer.

"He asked what I thought about pecans in the soup. He wants me to come over and help him finish his soup. I don't think pecans would go that well in soup."

What is she talking about? Tom thought, but before he could speak, Suzanne put her finger to his lips.

She lowered her face and kissed him on the forehead. "Nobody's going anywhere," she said, kissing him again, this time on the mouth. She put her hands in his hair and gazed at him for a few seconds, then kissed him lower on his neck.

"He's so full of himself," Tom mumbled.

He told her good night and rolled over and waited for her to ask him what was wrong, but she must have fallen asleep because the next time Tom realized what he was doing he was on his back staring at the light fixture in the middle of the ceiling. There was a haze around every blurred shape, the furniture fixed in no one place but hovering, capable of being moved by the slightest breeze or the gentlest touch.

He stirred again at the approach of dawn to find Suzanne standing before the open window with the curtain in her hand, and as he lay propped on one elbow watching her take shape in the emerging light, it unsettled him that he had nothing to say to her at all.

Tom awakened a few hours later and didn't bother to shower or shave. He left Suzanne sleeping and drove to the Zippy Stop on the corner, where he filled his small red gas-can and bought the *Worchester*

197

Sunday Telegram. When he backed the Cherokee into the garage, the street was quiet, the sun erasing the dew left by the night. He filled the Lawn King with gas, wanting to get started before Suzanne woke up. He wheeled the mower out of the garage, happened to glance up toward Dr. Gallant's house, and gasped.

Dr. Gallant was standing on the roof. His robe flapped behind him as he poured liquid from a bright red can onto the roof. Even from this distance, Tom could smell the gasoline, and saw the wet streaks along the shingles.

Dr. Gallant spotted Tom, and waved. "Top of the morning to you!" he called down. Tom noticed that he had shaved his moustache.

Suzanne was sitting at the kitchen table in boxers and an old T-shirt, sipping coffee, when Tom burst through the door. "I think I'll take the sports page—" she began, but he cut her off.

"Call the fire department!" he cried, and then Suzanne was out the door in her stocking feet. He followed her with the portable phone in hand, dialing for help. Before he could, he heard sirens, and hung up. A red car with flashing lights pulled up against the curb. The fire captain—the same deadpan woman from yesterday—hopped out in a navy blue uniform. She jogged across the lawn, the red lights spinning behind her. Two fire trucks, one with a huge ladder on top, pulled into the Gallants' driveway. Firemen jumped from both trucks. Neighbors were gathering on their lawns and porches.

The fire captain opened the Gallants' front door and disappeared inside, and as the door closed behind her, Tom looked up and saw his wife on the roof.

She was crawling along the ridgeline, away from Dr. Gallant, who was following her unsteadily. Suzanne made it to the chimney and stood using it for support.

"Zana!" Tom yelled, running across the lawn. Suzanne's hands were behind her against the bricks of the chimney as Dr. Gallant approached her, his hands outstretched like an airplane. He dropped the red container of gasoline. It bounced down the roof and came to rest in the tall grass. He reached Suzanne and tucked something into her boxers.

Firemen went in and out of the house as Dr. Gallant began to sing something to Suzanne, while one of Tom's neighbors across the street made a gun out of his fingers and shot himself in the head.

Tom couldn't imagine what was happening up there between them on that steep roof, but a cop stopped him before he could move any closer to the house. "Zana!" Tom shouted again. He imagined her slipping and rolling down the roof, or worse—Dr. Gallant catching her. Tom looked away in disgust.

Hoses in the back of the fire trucks looked like folded towels as Tom strolled past them, heading home. He bent over the Lawn King, primed its shiny engine, and snapped the cord. The mower shuddered and then caught life. Tom began to mow his grass. When he reached the property line, he continued into the tall grass beyond. Every so often, he looked up at the roof, but it was empty. Either they were inside the house together or had fallen from the roof together.

Tom would have mown until the Lawn King ran out of gas, but then a sports car pulled up behind one of the fire trucks. Tom stopped mowing, but kept his grip on the handle of the mower, letting go only when Mrs. Gallant stepped from the passenger side of the low-slung car, wearing the straw hat.

She was larger in the hips than he remembered, and up the driveway she went, pumping her arms, before a policeman stepped in her path. Foam shot from a hose to cover the gas-soaked shingles as the front door opened and Dr. Gallant stepped onto the porch. On one side of him stood the fire captain, on the other was Suzanne.

Tom ran up the hill to the house. He could see Dr. Gallant had changed into fresh, clean clothes, and his smooth upper lip made his face appear a decade younger.

"Mrs. Gallant," one of the policemen said to Suzanne.

"I'm she." Mrs. Gallant—the real one, not the imposter—nudged past Tom. A bead of sweat had frozen halfway down her face. She hugged her husband tightly, and the fire captain stepped back. Suzanne held her ground. "I've called Dr. Klepzig, Paulie. He's going to meet us at the station." She caressed the side of his head. "C'mon, I'll tell you all about my trip."

Dr. Gallant gazed warmly at his wife. "I'm afraid I ate all the leftovers."

The fire captain winked at Tom, then touched Dr. Gallant under the elbow. "Come on, Paul. Let's go."

Dr. Gallant tugged his arm away from her. "Romance, like a ghost, eludes touching. It's always where you were, not where you are."

"Let's go, Paulie," Mrs. Gallant said again, kissing her husband on the lips. She held his hand and the three of them stepped around Tom as if he were invisible.

"There's only one woman in the world, Tom," Dr. Gallant called over his shoulder. "She just wears different hats."

At the curb next to their mailbox, the Gallants piled into the back of a police car. They sped away, the lights of the car flashing silently. The hose slid backward through the grass by Tom's feet. Suzanne put her arm around Tom's waist. In her waistband was a folded piece of paper, but Tom didn't want to ask. He draped his arm around her shoulders, and as they lingered in the driveway, gazing at the departing fire trucks as if they were watching a sunset, Tom Boyd was happy.

The Cumulative Heron

In the fog, she hears the heron's croak,
the ship's horn,
some third sound.

Her maiden name begins with an S
not unlike the heron's neck, curves she hides
in her signature.

Through binoculars is not the same heron
from the fishing boat,
from beneath the surface.

When they married, neither had seen
a great blue heron or they didn't know they had
among other things.

She studied eloquence.
Now she puts stones in her mouth
to make a shore.

The heron walking like bamboo
is the heron hunkered in rain
is the ancient arrow.

As she drives home from the house of a dying friend
a heron flies obliquely across the road,
its shoulders hunched.

Of the 10,000 winds,
none troubles a feather
of the heron's ruff.

She reads many poems in which
there are herons. When she looks up, a silence
rests most of its weight on one dark leg.

What It Hinges On*

The white birds swirl above the water, pearls in a jar of airy oil, their name full of *L*s.

When she touches them: satin. When she smells her hand: sugared almonds. On her tongue: foam at the base of the waterfall.

Did she ever visit the Lake Country? She grew there. Did she drown in the water music that filled the chambers of her heart?

The birds were not pearls, but tiny hinged shells, bivalved, though not as the heart is valved.

Were they as beautiful as the full moon last night? someone asked. Not as loud, she answered, because the oil quieted the hinges.

That gold and sapphire vision has a specific meaning, someone said to her, "but I can't tell you yet."

Meanwhile, she was quicksilver—not the light but witness to the light.

The clock's ticking first murmured the word *eternity* one Sunday afternoon in October when she was seven.

She said she was going to get toe-shoes or go to medical school. To dance some new dance. Is that how it happened to Arthur Murray but he misinterpreted the dream?

She must go more slowly. Her dream of the high-ceilinged butterfly-shaped building, the *scriptum scriptorium*, might mean larva and cocoons, late silk, some third thing.

She has a watercolor voice. In these sweet, dangerous times, only biometrics can measure a life.

She lives in a jar; someone has poked holes in the lid and light comes in like night sky.

Da steh ich nun, ich armer Tor, und bin so klug, und bin so klug….

The door repeated, "It all hinges on," but she missed the last word.

———————————

*German phrases are from the opening scene of Goethe's *Faust*.

Bent and yet this nail
follows single file, slowly at first
breathing its way back

pulling the well closer—you lean over
as if one arch calms all the others
and between your jaws another nail

dangling: a lone death counted in the millions
so it will mean nothing and the spared hole
left empty for company, gathers around

where your lips must be, kept open
till the hammer brings water again
circling down and this floor takes in

the ice from some monstrous pile
already elbows, knees: rivers
unraveling to chase your hand away.

*

Forget the instructions, the walls
should be painted first
pulled upward so the ceiling

curves and the gloss
half white, half emptiness
—you don't see yourself yet

or how you grip the brush
with just one hand, the other
slack till a slow climbing turn

waits to be born, grasping for air
—trust as if the corners

were already hollowed out
and the room kept not yet dry
grown safe with purpose and cradle snow.

Epithalamium on a Theory of Gravity

for David and Lorena

The apple will fall to the Earth.

You may wake
to the cry of a child
in the night,
testing gravity, the pull
of one creature on another.

You may wake
to find your body
expanding, a solar system—
organs, ventricles, ribosomes,
intercostal constellations
orbit a bright, beating sun.

In the beginning,
heavy elements released by stars
became the planets,
became the body.

In the beginning
the adjective *gravis* meant heavy.
And *gravitas:* seriousness, dignity.

You may wake
to the heat of fusion,
your face toward the face
of a luminous other, two bodies,
inextricable binaries.

The Earth will fall to the apple.

Look out the window,
it's not the moon
pulling the tide
of this sea change.
It's not the moon
filling the room with light.

The Boar God's Breakfast

My horns have grown into my head
so I must ask, is this madness? Is
this? I lick the plate at home now
and soon will in town, dripping along
the linen cloths, over spilling
the wine. My teeth, knocked queer in a fall
rattle their sockets, assume new positions
point north, point south, or seek the earth,
kingdom of worms and cool rest.
I swallow and fill my gut with bone.

"My Funny Valentine"

how can I sleep   here, where   like azure—water   *Chet Baker—*
—*anyone*   breathing—*throaty*, or not,   *"My*
sleep—with you   *rough*,   not like water   *Funny Valentine"*

here, this pillow   *suspends*   —enough to   —*drifting, drifting,*
on which—of   *the palates*—cannot know, we are   *bodies, numb to*
which, geese   find time, I   awake—   *all feeling, moody*

and down   assume, we   *float like*   —such blue
—our heads rest,   are one.   *angels*—   his fingers on
your hair,   voiceless   in aquarium   the trumpet, *the needle?*

black—*streetlight?* —I cannot find   —find light   *Amsterdam? heroin?*
moon?—   friction, enough   to turn—*halogen*   the voice
beside me now?   for speech.   —our colors on.   chameleonlike.

Relations in the Difficult World

Tectonics might explain it, but from here—a distance
Only finger-steps from anywhere—I like to think

Of ours as mutual agreement, a sort of parting gesture
That says "this is the natural order of things—

We've moved on. Here are your books. Here is your hat,
Your tropical climate & 58 inches of annual rainfall.

Write if you find time."—& though we can't, I think,
Entirely recall these lives together, or remember

What it was that caused those first small fractures
To compound & slip, spidering like ancient tributaries

Through dry bone, perhaps, each day
A little more comes back: the coagulation of calls

From distant birds, wind & rain, reach down, sink in.

And what would you have me do? From here—
With my fingers residing in Lima, my wrists, twisted

Toward the South Pacific, its tepid, blue water
And brilliant diffractions of surgeonfish, holding my body

In a dead-man's float—I can hold my breath
Nearly forever, look up & out, & know the world.

Osip Mandelstam
A Transit Camp, Siberia, 1938

I

crystal fog
pink snow on the ice fields
in the night

I dream of elm leaves pulsing
with color in the trees
I reach for them

the leaves
become white rags
I try to sew

the leaves into pages
but the slender threads
fall away from my hands

I look for a way to find ink
from red berries but the *oblepikha*
bush bleeds in my fingers

now neither hand can write
a rough-legged hawk
flies overhead

the pale wing beats fade
into clouds and when I wake
I write this in my mind

I memorize the ice fields
at the faint sound of my heart
I recall the razor in my shoe

but fail to use it
I think of the hope my wife has
the hope in silent words

II

am I real and
will death
ever come

it is easier to taste
the pale bread
of paper than the heavy

blood of ink
if I write in short breaths
unlike I used to

it is because
I count more
moments than hours

more hours than days
of someone else's hope
Forgive me

III

for what I am
telling you some day
my words will come

to you in snow the unwritten ones
you will transcribe them
in the bleak sun

of your own winter we are alike
fast in our chain links our secrets
I predict my voice

will come to you on the days
when you lose heart and need
a witness most you may find only

a faint placing of words
forgive me
my mind must be the paper now

but come back for me
imaginary scribe
tell all about the fields

returning in the vast spring
with the rowan and the larch
and the flowers of every color

Nudes and Bathers

"I like painting best when it looks eternal."
—*Pierre-Auguste Renoir*

I've lived with Renoir for a year now
in this room
where luminous women hold small flowers.
They look related,
sisters or cousins,
though it isn't so.
He had no interest in precise reproductions.
It was the light he wanted
coming through them.
     In the next gallery
a grandmother admires a Van Gogh.
Did you ever study this artist?
The granddaughter shakes her head, stares into the green
face of a woman with fat knuckles,
ochre nails, background the dark
green wallpaper of a mind breaking down
into manic dots and flowers, vines
and pinwheels. The child screams—
       She's looking at me—
hides behind the grandmother's skirt.
A young man strides past them
as if reeled in by Renoir's red-haired girl.
I've watched so many men walk up to her.
They can't seem to get close enough,
standing there like supplicants
waiting for her to notice them,
to speak.
    I could sit here all day, listen
to the offerings,
the small prayers of breath,

each piece revealing more,
the way you get to know someone,
or try to over time, and without thinking
imprint every gesture and expression
through the lens of your desire.
What eye comes to a picture wanting nothing?
                                        I was always the one at parties
trying to get the shots, my nieces
making faces, waving me away,
my son flipping me the bird.
They didn't realize
this was a way to save ourselves,
to look back from some unknown future
into our happiness—
                        At least that's what I told myself,
crouched beside the sofa,
or hidden in a corner aiming
to lift them out of context,
turn them into something I could understand.
                                I don't take photos anymore.
No record of my lover
tucking one strand of hair behind my ear
when we made up;
no snapshot of my son
hugging me goodbye at the airport in Frankfurt.
I'll have to do without
because I'm in them,
though I admit the softness time gives to a moment
can be holy.
                Today three years ago,
I sat beside my father's body.
I have to close my eyes to picture him,
expressionless, his mouth sewn shut.
I wanted to lay my head on his chest,
but he looked so real—

Where would Renoir go for the light in this tableau,
a dull alcove where the legs of a steel table show
beneath the red blanket—
not the father's name, but the funeral home's
stitched into its weave.
Where would he focus for beauty?
The daughter's head bent forward,
her hair falling into a mass of red;
or her hand, tentative,
tucking the edge of a blanket under her father's chin,
his face made up,
refusing light?
I can't help myself,
intruding on their silence,
looking for a pulse in the stillness
of his lashes,
the way her shoulders shiver
as she turns her back to me.

Harbor

Out of littered sidewalks and subways, into
centuries-old gardens of fern and begonia,
strawberries served on Royal Copenhagen.
In what language could she tell

Scovrider Due about the pinched
little berries packaged in plastic
back at the A&P?
How could she admit or with

what words say: she never had
her own bedroom, that cancer
turned her father miserly,
how she wore that green uniform

the color of worn out dollar bills
bagging groceries at the Daitch Shopwell,
saved the money, hid the application,
and the scholarship was a miracle.

In Denmark, of all countries in the world
a Jewish girl on her own could be safe
even if the story about King Christian
wearing a star of David to defy the Nazis

was a myth. In W. W. II the Danes smuggled out
their Jews. There really were red roofs with
nests of storks, cobblestone streets,
and a cottage in Odense where

Hans Christian Andersen composed the dark,
instructive tales Disney turned into
happily ever after. If only "The Ugly Duckling"
were really a swan, if only "The Little Mermaid"

could dance like that Yonkers girl who ran
bare-legged into the North Sea, after a Danish boy
named Jorgen covered her face and neck with kisses.
But who was she kidding?
In Copenhagen Harbor, the naked mermaid was fused
to a rock. Back at Alexander's Department Store
on the Grand Concourse, she'd be jostling for
girdles heaped like flounder on the bargain table,

opening Jorgen's letters. Unable to answer
the easiest question, How are you?
A prune danish, a cheese danish — her life.
Mermaid with legs, every step inland searing.

Glissan O

Glissan o caterpillar name with the letter
eaten out like a leaf-hole
or a piano with a deadened key,
the delicate glissando with a mute note,
a broken harpsichord string snapped
from too much passion. Caterpillars
have taken over your garden, swallowtails
perhaps, though the guide doesn't give
tomatoes as a host plant for anything—
mottled duskywings or bog coppers,
fritillaries, goatweeds, sawgrass skippers,
names that I offer as if they meant something,
not knowing if they leave traces when they split
their skin or if their anterior barb stings.
I touched lightly the stinger, grazing its tip,
as you would deaden a string to reach its harmonic—
pingggg an octave higher shimmering tone.
Yet I must confess music wasn't on my mind—
red caterpillar thorn something you did not want
to brush in the morning when you water—
but the music lingers. Baroque harp tunes
that seem to accord with the runners and suckers
of profuse plants, all blending together
until you cannot separate one from the other.
Planxtys of a blind harpist, caterpillar song.
They greet you as sentinels at dawn
and quickly disappear—though they remain
stationary, only the angle of vision alters
or they withdraw the gift of their visible nature.
I think of their presence as grace,
the simple fact of their existence a benediction,
though they make harvesting a trial for you

and our neighbors tell of dowsing caterpillars
with gasoline and setting them ablaze,
and how could I tell them of fiery salamanders
and the King and Queen coiled in the grave,
marriage of sulfur and quicksilver,
and the green chrysalis jewel-shimmer
or cream of conch shell suspended by silk thread
that we've not yet found hidden in the leaves.
I think of them as milkweed pods so heavy
they pull their stalks to the ground—
touch them and they might burst.
Doesn't milkweed attract butterflies?
Elemental affinities. I think of gifts
as scatterings, releasing each thing to its destiny,
as when wings open to release their startling
colors as a warning or when morning glories
obscure the garden's recesses, twisting along stalks
until the caterpillars vanish, leaving black traces
that we pray are the first signs of the emerging chrysalis.

Stations of the Cross

On Eric Gill's crucifix the letters swarm
And collapse, their very clarity transfigured
Into a thorn bush. Peer into that white
Expanse where the body resides
I pull back from Christ's torso, smooth
As driftwood, his groin ravaged by gulls.
But I am dragged into its suffocating
purity, its obsessive grandeur.
Over and over the same letters:
Forms once bird wings and spear-points,
Seedballs, horns rubbed clean of velvet.
To inscribe letters in stone must be to wrestle
With the angel of bereavement.
I sense the life surge in these letters as they flee.
Crack the bones of syllabry and read their patterns.
I see Christ's body floating in the surf.
His mouth and eyes are caked with salt.
His hair falls downward like tentacles.
Christ's naked form does not meet your eye.
It erects a space that cannot be traversed.

When will I not succumb to the enigma of purity,
When will I cease to dream of broken terracotta nudes
That flake and collapse in the fire.
Once I would like to gather these images
Like figs fallen from the tree
And let them dissolve on my tongue.
Then they would seem less elusive, like a dead bird
Cupped in your hand, weightless and hollow,
Or a pear whose skin has become soft.
Once I would like to celebrate the infidelity of clay.
Once I would like to sing of torsos asleep in their perfume,

Intoxicated by their own collapse, trace furtive truths
Of your body submerged in the bath,
Of your knees and face transformed to water-lilies,
Of your breasts turbulent as fish in shallow water.
But it is an idle dream: I know you would turn away
If I asked to model your body in all its vulnerability.
You sense the arrogance of Yahweh breathing life
Into dust, ignoring the moisture escaping
From its folds. It is good that clay splinters
In the fire—serenity would destroy us.

Ferlinghetti Midnight

Run   run to catch up with the historical Jesus
                 Indian filmmakers   sun-dried cuisine
try   *only the dead are disengaged*
              is it too late are we running out of swordfish
                   they're logging Canada
don't get off the highway

but choose   Marxist or feminist
     and I am waiting

your body can be your friend
         alkaline soil can be amended
            people surf for a good used Volvo
   for a religious revival
   to sweep thru the state of Arizona

                  the watch he gave you for Christmas
                  may still be back at the house
it looks so small

it must be your glasses
braces ought to be considered if only for the lowers
              do your abs   you may need to re-enter the market
read up on stocks
consider Prague next summer   New Guinea's best for birding

you have to get chorizo on the east side   everyone knows Maytags

don't look like a fool   personal shoppers are available

        if only we could believe our children won't suffer

with the right clinic you can avoid most risks get a top-of-the-line baby
sleep through the night

Amniocentesis

In ancient Greece, the *amnion's*
a sacrificial plate to hold
a victim's blood. Four millennia

from that naming, I'm watching
a computer screen enlarge her
amniotic sac, the swirl of albumin

and pyin, the unfinished form
of our unnamed child. I'm watching
the hollow needle pierce the skin,

slide toward the womb, suck in
the solution that will tell us
the child's a healthy child.

If it's not, will it bear a name,
or become victim to bloody fate?
And what solution will wash

that speck of flesh and blood
from our hands? Four millennia
haven't cleansed us. The doctor

marshals the evidence, enlarges
the screen, reveals its watery home.
Floating. Restless. We're inside.

A white explosion
where the hollow needle strikes.
The foetus kicks and slaps

its uncompleted limbs.
This bright intrusion might be
a burning star, for all it knows,

a spent cinder hissing into the inner sea
from four millennia away.
There'll be no definite sighting.

Perhaps a memory of surprise.
A strange glimmer in the dark.
A first visit from another planet

where darkness alternates with light
and words abort their meanings
one generation at a time.

Mistress Lasiren Shipwrecks the Slaveship *Inspiration*

1.

High tide spits out a mermaid, caught
in the purgatory damp, beached
where waves break against black sand, hot
with charcoal swirls and fire coils. At sea,
many of her people drown, amongst
those who are not their kin. Beware,
though ancestors warn with their last gasps, she flicks
her tail dismaying guardians of the reef, unaware
that she could be plucked from the shallows
where she watches the middle passage in her hand-held mirror
combs through the seaweed of her hair, glows
in the afternoon light, sipping blues through a perforated straw.
The bugle sounds her feast day; conch shells litter the sand.
And still she splashes, unable to resign herself to liquid or to land.

2.

The Jews begged the United States to bomb
The trains that sped them to homes advertised
In the ghetto, relocation to the impending doom.
You could say it was a surprise
Horrified, America declined to engage
Turned back ships spilling over with Europe's refuse
Closed their shores until Pearl sparked their rage
Those ships sailed 1/3 of the triangle currents. Bemused
Schools of sharks familiar with the depths to which men sink
Drew lots on who would capture the first to dive
Perhaps the passengers glimpsed the Siren's wink
the flash of scale before the torpedo struck side
How long did it take sharks to recognize
In the flesh of their prey, the subtle taste of genocide.

3.

Was it a domestic dispute that provoked
La Sirene to trail her serpentine fingers in deeper waters?
To compose an aria that would deafen even the ears of the cargo
An answer to a prayer uttered within the belly of that ill-christened vessel
As it lumbered through the last lei, one plea
Carried above the din and touched her volatile heart
Without informing her lover, Admiral Agwe
She sang a dreadful symphony, so sweet
The gulls wailed a chorus, the dolphins chortled
The refrain beckoned the lower decks to dive
Those with wings flew back to Ginen, alive.
Offering their backs to survivors, the turtles paddled
To shore, and from behind her parasol, Ezili dipped
Her heels in waters perfumed with foreign blood, skipped.

Note: Lasiren, or *La Sirène*/the Siren, is also known as Ezili of the Waters.
She is part of the pantheon of *loas,* or spirits, in Haitian Vodou. Portrayed on
Vodou flags as a mermaid, she is also represented by *Caridad del Cobre* (Our
Lady of Charity).

Beach Stone

Too smooth and comely
　　　to be rock, which says
　　　　　hard edges, sharp

intent, this sweet weight
　　　hefted in the hand
　　　　　fits curve of palm

like a breast, small loaf,
　　　a cool thought from
　　　　　water's deep intelligence.

Who can know
　　　the language
　　　　　of this ancient

tribe, its former
　　　speech of stars
　　　　　and firmament

hardened by contracting
　　　earth into one long
　　　　　vowel of silence.

Imagine its fiery
　　　plummet through
　　　　　the spark and fuse

of beginning, the slow
　　　cooling, descent
　　　　　into gravity, becoming

earth. Creamy flesh now
　　　rubbed and tumbled
　　　　　by the ravishing

arm of the wave.
       To come ashore,
              to lie cobbled among

one's neighbors
       bleeding the common
              colors, to grow

fainter and less distinct,
       losing oneself bit by bit,
              becoming every

footprint
       on every beach
              might be enough.

Harbor

It was a summer we never spent
at the Cape together, a shoreline
I roughly imagined, bluffed
from the curves of our young bodies.
It was a rowboat I didn't climb
gingerly into. Had we pushed

away from the dock, lips
of water may have curled
around the hull. Had we plunged
our two oars into the water.
But what oars? What water?
We faced each other

and didn't. The harbor,
even the idea of the harbor,
is lost. We may as well have been
dreaming, hardly fathoming
the years we never spent,
not rowing and not rowing.

Moses

Leaving him with little more
than prayers that the pitch
would hold, his mother

hoped another would take him
from the river into her slender,
sunned arms, and name him.

Where will I be when you
open your drowsy mouth
to another's breasts as soft

as fresh figs, as though your
first breath is of her skin?
Far off as myth, lamenting

locks of your hair the birds
refuse to bring me out of loyalty
to her? What will I call you then?

Not love, but a memory
of loving. What a quiet
concession: a mother calling

her son by the name
another had chosen, *Moses,*
meaning *drawn from the water.*

Certain Things Should Not Be Mentioned Versions 1 & 2

I am not about the fire, the goddamn fire.
But let's/do begin/to talk about
the ash. Balanced, tender, a story in its own
telling.
She is captured, held there/not waiting
for next breath/next collapse.
She speculates something of winter and distance and of recovery.
The woman so heavy with memory makes wild
outrageous motions—hair swinging
side to side, reckless.
The tangles are reckless and on the run.
If they could speak, they would say *we are*
your only escape.
Again: no fire. Only hair half soaked in ash.
Color/blends/ruins.

From the River's Edge

Is it poetry to say that each time I cross over a
certain bridge on the Yellowstone, I remember the way
green vinyl felt on the back of my legs instead of how
my own mother's feet, stiff from death, felt in my hands?
I did not know that a poet could feel words rising from
drops of sweat around her knees. Or that what my palms
pressed against was only silence. Can a poet speak of a
second version of her mother? The one who lives in a
silent cave where she allows no visitors, gives no interviews.
Her memoir is being written there by a shadow seven feet
tall that can hold no pen or pencil, both hands missing.
My living mother dreams of new waters that have no
adequate translation.

We Two

When he was being born,
      I floated above the women
who held my legs
      open.

There was a sea
      below us, airy and bright,
and such momentum
      as he rose,
I sank
      and rose again.

White effluence tossed us
      without sound,
we exhaled into water and mist.

I longed to stay this way,
      indwelling,
near a clear shallow.

Squalls, a sheet pulled against
      skin and
we breathed in electric light.

Selves torn,
      we slept,
marrow closing over gill.

Emilie Singing

Emilie shook out a towel over short sea grasses,
her arms moving and parting like tawny reeds.

She unwrapped a white sarong from around her hips
and we lay down like sisters to sleep and I saw

the morning shadows fine-drawn across her abdomen.
I curled to the center of my heart to hear her breathe.

When she was pregnant with Ange, I gave her lavender sachets.
Her husband kissed her neck and pulled up her gauze blouse

so I could place my palm over the acorn-brown belly.
My emerald ring caught the edge of her blouse, unraveling a long thread.

In early winter, Emilie gave birth to her tiny daughter
who died wrapped warm atop her mother's stomach,

breath of a glacier lily slowly tapering from blue, blue fingernails.
They would not let anyone take her away at night, so they slept

while she lay between them until a light like water
shimmered across the hospital floor and Emilie said, *It's time.*

When she called, I could not speak for knowing
that sometimes she would travel alone in dawn wind singing

for that which her heart still loved,
falling like a bird through the sparse material of sky.

A Fat Sestina

I follow my friend up a curving trail, 350 pounds
weighing me down. He is no more than 120. I look up,
(always look up), to see the back of his hooded sweatshirt and two
Chuck Taylor feet leading me to this Lookout Point,
a place where the view is worth cardio respiratory failure.
He says it's an easy walk. He is known to lie.

My whole life I have lied
about my size, the extra pounds
that cling around the circle of my knees, that bunch at the neck. I failed
to tell the DMV my actual weight. But as she looked me up
and down, her pointed
smirk prompted me to say, *Give or take one or two.*

And when I stood on the treadmill that demanded my weight, I pressed two-
hundred twenty-eight, what I was in eighth grade, when I used to lie
down on the school's blue mats and wait for the second hand to point
to twelve. I'd start pounding
my back onto the mat, sixty-two sit-ups
in a minute. I never failed

to impress Coach Chandler, a portly man who never saw me as a fat failure.
In the mirror, I molded my stomach into two,
lifted my flab up
and let it drop. I'd lie
flat on the bed, suck in my gut, try to hide the pounds,
let the fat spread like water. That's the point.

Fatigue steals my breath as my friend stops on the grassy trail to point
at mushrooms sprouting up trees—like clams. I fail
to notice. Nature loses its brilliance—a mossy log just an obstacle I pound
my knee on, the sweet smell of a drizzle tainted by my deep gasps of

gnats. Two
spotted toads avoid my lumbering steps. Not much further, he lies.
The trail narrows and a spray-painted arrow points up

the steepest incline of the hike, up
through thick hickories I stumble and lean on. I am at the point
of collapse, surrendering to this mountain, lying
down in this mud trodden path, giving into my failing
body. I watch my friend disappear around the bend of two
cedars. My heart pounds

from my toes up to my pulsating temples. I will not stop, will not fail
to reach Lookout Point and see the gray rippling lake below. I am already
                there, the two
of us lying lightly on the grass, the sun melting away like a pound of butter.

from Archaeology

(For the people involved in excavations of village and cave sites along the Rio Talgua, at the western edge of La Mosquitia Natural Reserve, near Catacamas, Honduras, June 1996.)

1.

Every morning the air burns
The mangoes rock on their stems
as the same cat climbs to the same roof
where broken tiles are caught in a rusting gutter
Who lives here where morning means smoke
and afternoon means smoke
and evening is meaner than smoke
harder than any native wood?
Machetes take root in hands
scars bloom on trees where mangoes
hang like christmas balls
ornaments to the rainy season
plumb lines to the southern cross
Not every machete strikes the courtyard tree
Not every bottle ends up broken, embedded
in the garden wall   Not all poverty
bares its swollen belly
in the shrunken arms of a weathered mother

2.

In the courtyard of the hotel
ficus trees grow in concrete boxes
Grass struggles in the ashen dirt
spreads itself thin to survive
Ants flourish in refuse too small to see,
drops of beer, crumbs from corn cakes,
the trail of leavings that could show us
where we have been and how we are stuck
There must be an instrument that can plot
the bits of trash we drop along the way:

in a photo taken from an airplane
see the shiny paths cross and merge
leading always
back to the slick ponds of slag
the concentrations
we bog in

6.

The shape of things that have lost their usual form:
voices echo in the empty hall   speech
with no meaning   rhythms of talk   whimsical
imitations   like the cadence of wind
the cackle of chickens in the yard
Hollow words   shells of pure sound
stumble in waves and bursts   unselective
undirected   into this ear   that wall
inevitably   not by choice
not by chance   but because
inevitably is the way sound travels:
Juan Carlos Hotel   Talgua Cave
hangar tucked among the hills
near Tegucigalpa: language before history
before words were words
the shape of sound   traveling alone

9.

Three thousand years of lying dead,
growing soft and bloated,
a starchy kernel moved once a century
by floods or goofy bats,
touched most by the hair on spider legs,
the drip from limestone ceilings.
What is a tooth,
loose and safe for so long,
or a village
after fifteen hundred years of putting on mud and manure,

burrowing down?
An eternity of connections is built and spoiled
and built again, differently.
How old are ideas?
How absolute is longing?

With watch and chain we mark minutes,
while shadows play upon us:
      a chill in the cave's dead air
      light looming purple over the field:
counting seconds, mapping degrees,
      words meticulously exchanged at a corner table
      cruelties thrown across a room, a bed, a nation
What rule or cup can keep time
in its sensible, transparent grasp?
Listen: here come the quiet people,
the ones who move into the hills
just before the clocks are wound
just before the hammer falls
What kind of musician can bear
a metronome that sputters,
that rushes then slows,
when the hands are busy
already
making music?

10.

Watch the mirror
Cover the clock
See if you can stop the happening
that seems uncontrollable,
Altogether we are accidental
and our effect is like grey dishwater
tossed into the red gravel road
dispersed   uneven
evanescent
under the white sun

12.

Carlos Rodriguez in black letters.
Omar Was Here in red. Names
on rocks, notches in a tree. A lizard
runs on bowed legs across the path
into the flush of leaves, wild cards
of every suit scattered across
the moss floor. Above me,
vines sprout from treetops, the rain
pecks at the forest. A chainsaw whines
on the next mountain, a shrill complaint
carried leaf to leaf, in open palms,
across the Talgua, through coffee bushes
and plantains, up the washed trail
to here.
           Natural or not, these images fill me,
feed me: the earth, the ways we use it.
Native or not, I am here, climbing,
planting my boots one at a time
among these complicated roots,
short of breath, but deeply alive.
It's curious: these upright lizards,
these roots in the ground below
and in the canopy above,
the places that feel familiar
but can't be.
           I am native, natural—or not—
half expecting to be ambushed
standing here in history's way,
tribe of one, perfectly alone,
one of a familiar tribe,
lost, curiously at home.

18. (Documentary)

Rum, ice, airplane glue. A smoke ring
for every promise kept waiting. Hardly the script

he had hoped for, wobbly, convulsive, vanishing
with a wheeze. Still, the american producer will
shoot to the end, blowing promises like kisses,
an unstrung kite wheeling from wind to wind,
crewboys in tow. He'll damn the whore who
brought him to this, remembering vacantly
how on a torpid June day he walked
among the sultry workers, greeting them loudly
in his own language, becoming one with them
under the sun: pointing, laughing, cursing
with pleasure, rolling the ice in his tall, sweating glass.

20.

for the field workers

How does it feel to burn
for us
who have lived our days in the caves
of privilege
where heat and sun are pinched off softly
by the earth's crooked throat
and our voices are served
separately
on trays of rich silence?
Your skin blisters   your hands ache
as you dig deeper into every day
in the white glare of details
picking through rocks and dirt
for broken bits of history
You sweat with conviction
proud and bitter
Stare the sun down in its hottest eye
if you think such a duel diminishes us

But where are the ordinary angles of the sun
in this zone of absolute darkness
of artificial stone-washed light?

How will we tell the tone of the wind
in a tomb where nothing stirs,
where no rock bends
or gives to touch?
And will we come out the same,
to the same forest and rooted paths
that brought us to this shelter?
Or will we emerge to a burnt mound,
destruction that feeds
on the feet and hands of children,
the village in ruins again?

23.

What is sky but the place in its own light?
Sunset is different here, the stars fall harder.
Day stretches tighter, bending on shrinking tendons.

Polish the air to silver-blue and every dry blade
gets up from its bed, stands on hidden shoulders.
Call down the storm clouds, dark musty pillows,
and watch the field go bladeless, one sea rocking,
beating back its rising brow. Now a man comes
running, splashing toward the sullen farmhouse, the wind,
the rain, no mountains at all, a narrow place,
violent, right. If the lightning strikes him,
he will never speak fast or dream for himself again;
caught in the cloudy brains of must, traveling
the line without end, words spark off, late and low,
and the same deck of dreams is cut to everyone
stunned in the field, dealt from the sky,
the place in an eerie light, down the drunken wire.

24.

Barbed wire, rusty bodies,
shards of glass on tops of walls.
Move in a country that stands still

and risk cutting yourself to the bone.
Danger lines the road,
tetanus stands upended in the ditch
as the bus slips on mudrock
toward the cliff's edge.
Anachronisms dwell in every house:
wood-burning oven, hands to harvest corn,
a TV for fascinating the naked boy.
Warps of time and tool tend the field:
machetes clear the scrub brush
while computers graph the phase of seismic waves
pounded into the thorny ground.
On the bent rim of this frontier town
anomalies underground and above
put on a terrible circus; an absurd company,
entrenched, corrupt, pitches its gaudy tent
for a long, prosperous run. Amid the din
a ceiba tree stands huge in the town square,
unsung, dumb with solitude and memory,
a root for every townsperson's twisted heart.
Seek the public art and *you* will find none
(unless this grim comedy be art).
Seek the poets and *for you* they are gringos
who have taken on Spanish names
for clean shame and the liberty of exile.
Can art move in a land out of whack,
a land of machetes and soap operas
where the washed out roads drag their ragged hems
up the mountains to borders marked by blood
and buried mines; or is it only a phantasm of forgetting,
another cartoon, that haunts ruins, old and new?
Every day you ride the rust in the back of the speeding pickup
running the gauntlet of sharp edges and broken things,
looking for signs in the streets, in the eyes
of men and women walking to town, in the hands
of the stall-keepers hanging meat, listening
for the quiet truer stories, and you know

the danger is not in sharp objects, mean sideshows,
but in the stiffening back, the numb fingers,
the dull edges of your own starved, art-forsaken eye.

25.

What would it mean if you cut your best vein here
in a country where archaeology bows its head
keeping its nose to the ground
a mythical beast   half human   half dirt
a Honduran back with gringo hands
an odd body tied to the twitching tail
of progress and publicity?
In a patois of competing interests
badly phrased   barely comprehensible
it offers the past as the future—
bags of red bones raised on display
in the town's only library
cans of hot Coke lowered by a camera boom
to barefoot boys in the cow field
knowledge for everyone's and no one's sake.
Meanwhile, across town medicine arrives with god
from Utah . . .
What would it say   about you
about it all   if you wrung poetry
from a sour bandanna?
Weeks of sweat collected in a handkerchief
ordinary sweat
made in Honduras   not Memphis or Rome
cheap sweat
the dew from the everyday brow.
Say it straight, then—
we were there   you   me
there we were   everyone
together   vulnerable   heads bowed
eyes on the ground
shouldering the dead weight of unplotted time

searching in the gap-toothed skull of our own memories
for lost keys   our own imperatives
our fading fluency at love.
These are the stubborn tools
symptoms of history
of poverty—mine   ours—
and more   slow themes
denied a scene in the official reel
where beasts dance, transformed.
But here they are: stageless   unannounced.
So what *does* it mean to cut vein over
the grey dirt of another country
surrounded by another language
drawn to the writing on the garden wall?
Ojo Vidrio No Tocar:
look out   glass   do not touch
You'll throw your clean bandannas
into the crowd of street children
and take your leave
hesitant   anxious
wondering what shape repair will take
and how to bear the accident
you've been avoiding
and preparing for all your life—
this new body its best vein spoken for
already dripping
ordinary   rhythmic
marking the route home
and the hard way back
to the country
of sharp rust
grey dirt
bright mornings carried in the rooster's mouth.

Near the Yangtze River

Heavy-lidded from her opium years and unflinching
love for rice wine, she kneels beside the dark periphery
of water, unable to stop staring at the squatting monk
beneath the tree across the river, how this odd, brown-

robed man cups air in hands, lifts it like a round
of melon to his lips, a ritual drinking, perhaps,
but one this woman does not—cannot—understand.
Broken-hearted, she slumps face-first into the water,

wondering if this time she has the nerve to die. Alone
now, she no longer hears the call of magic. She no longer
sees sunset upon the burial mounds of her ancestors.
Her future is as easy to read as rocks spilled from

a bag of prophecy. When she yanks her head out,
water running down her nose, her throat, it's the monk
who's watching her, a simple mirror of expectation;
in this moment, she feels the four slow wings of moon

and stars, remembers how, as a girl, she thought the night
sky was a jolly fat man's bulging shirt, the steady constellations
as buttons that refuse to burst open. She dunks her head once
more, deep, letting current warmth sew her back together.

Lieder

No. 1
My man sits on the sofa
listening to Schubert.
I've had hunks and torsos
in my time, with lots of hair,
the kind who really do gleam
but eventually to run to fat.
He is not that.
My hero, I say. He cooks for me
and folds the laundry.
I am a front-stoop dreamer
reading the Sanskrit of birdsong
and the runes of leaves
against a blue sky.

Because I love ecstacy
and grandeur, my man
takes me on tours
through the anterooms of lieder.
Then on, into the spacious
emotional mess of opera.

No. 2
At a reception in a church basement
I sat across from a widow.
We ate potato salad and discussed men,
while mine, in red suspenders
and baggy dungarees, wandered the crowd.
The widow said she could never go
for a man who was too feminine,
with sideways looks at the red suspenders.
She said a man who cooks

and cleans and fusses around
in my turf would get in the way.
It would be like going to bed
with the maid. Maybe then
her dearly departed did just that
for forty years, but it didn't seem
respectful to say so. Instead
I hummed a bit of the Mahler song
about a tea house on a bridge,
the whole scene reflected
upside down in the water.
It cleared my head.

No. 3
Once my man's heart foofed out
and he had to have new hoses put in.
He's got a zipper on his chest
and a seam up one leg,
three deep round scars
on his belly, from the drains.
I touch them with my finger tips,
stroking ocean ripples or the mysterious
purple horizon of mountains
that mark the skyline
between here, and there.

He loves to touch my breasts
because they are small and soft:
sparrows, skylarks, he says.
He likes to hold my face in his hands.

When they opened his rib cage
they found songs
from Das Lied von der Erde,
Mahler's Eighth Symphony,

and the entire Ring. There were also
finches and cardinals, some puffins,
a pair of blue-footed boobies
doing a mating dance,
some endangered species, a quetzal,
an emerald toucanet.
They were left undisturbed
so that when we kiss
they fly between his rib cage
and mine, singing and nesting,
fluttering in both of our bodies.

THE RIGHT DIFFUSION OF HISTORY AND LONGING AT THE FALLOW NEXUS OF BOTANY, COMMERCE, PHYSICS, AND UNPREDICTABLE DESIRE

Following the path the moon makes on the turnpike I meet trees
    for the first time: the length of them, I mean, not abstracted
        from xylem or phloem, panicle or leaf but all the more intimate

For parallel vectors sending the last rays of evening sun
    pinging out between us like glass beads on a tablet, like glass
        beads about to be released from a trader's leather pouch, snug

In that holt then passed hand to greasy hand in the dapple
    of the clearing trust makes. The moon has seen this, she understands
        a bad bargain whispering again to the space beyond the twin

Drums where balance is maintained, where particles one step
    up from the atomic rise and fall and rise in scripted mediation
        between what is known and what is not, curve of the earth

And solid ground packed underfoot in August heat, the haggling
    in languages some want to believe are mutually exclusive.
        Therefore calque. Therefore the coined word, lingua franca

Radiating into pidgin as the immune system of one party fails,
    starting with the vowels—the consonants broadening—smoothing
        out into a kind of onionskin, translucent.

By then there's a house standing with glazed panes separating
    each window from its function. I call to you from behind one
        but you're ten, a hundred, a thousand miles away.

Night falls and the moon whispers Love, as she does,
    skimming over the treetops so that each leaf moans half-awake
        from its photosynthetic dream, stirring in the warm

Breath of a breeze the same way flesh in its second sleep
　　comes faintly to itself when touched, when nudged not quite
　　　　to the limen of external genuflection: I open the window

And the breeze comes to me too, and I moan with the leaves, a little:
　　shutting my eyes and pressing my hands to the lids until the phosphenes
　　　　begin their command performance, moire of pale cream shifting

Into violet as if the spectrum could be keeping more than mathematics
　　from us, that cold logic with its synaesthetic sheen. The moon sinks lower
　　　　beneath the trick of perception distance confers, still troubling

The fresh buds at the tips of the sugar maples which reach out
　　asking what it is she wants and how much it will cost, they would
　　　　pay anything, surely a betrayal is at hand—this moon

Will return tomorrow with her bill set down crazed in blood
　　like a treaty, any torn indenture, the only bargain I can live up to,
　　　　easy as sap rising now. This time I promise. I'll try.

SKYLAND BOULEVARD

In the dream we all left one another
for discrete communions, though overlapping
in minor details of the spirit—a hatbrim,
say, fringe of black or gray on a winter coat.
When we saw one another in the street
it was with a kind of frank sadness, as if
we had known all along it would come to this.
Waking, the room seemed brighter
than the word refurbished would otherwise
have suggested. Outside the rain had stopped.
I walked down to where the chain stores
clustered by the freeway, bought a paper, a Coke,
half a sandwich. On the way back
I noticed a footpath leading into the scrub pines
behind the grocery. That same tired argument:
repentance, *metanoia* in the Greek,
the body's thick coresidence, the mind's
allegiance misconstrued. I boarded the noon train
with over-the-counter barbiturates in my left
pocket, knowing all too well the stops and hard-worn
stations on the red-eye through north Georgia,
around me every present touch or polite
intimation either collapsing or, like the light,
flying helpless and helplessly apart.

After Mastectomy

for my mother

In the pueblo of the body, the body of mud
and sticks, rain gets in, structures dissolve,

what isn't supposed to happen does. Stranger
cells invade houses of milk, a woman descends

into anesthetic silence, sews a quilt from petals
of her body. Tonight something holds me here,

makes me stay inside what hurts. Islands pass by
and I run a treadmill towards them—wish for

the somewhere I am not, for the absent, for the lost.
As the scars heal over, she will grow a garden, a green

room of vines and sunlight. We will walk without shoes
counting breaths, sleep naked with grass between

our toes. We will bare the instruments of our bodies
to the moon and say play, we have nothing to hide.

The Laundry, *"La Lavandería"*

San Miguel de Allende, Mexico

Were it not for the reluctance of water,
hands aching against the light in the courtyard,
I could feel the tips of my fingers,
that desire for touch and persistence,
so much ritual that it could have become
another pleasure I would come to.
Here, where the sweet rain
offers its clean tongue across my face
in the midst of this endless chore–
a shake, tug, then twist.
It's as if an instant of light and air stills
and I remember *The Jardin,*
scent of wood and stone, each doorway
opening to cobblestone streets.
So much mystery
that it could have been any other country
but this, it was
the only time I wore the dress.
There, where the faces of taxi drivers
and even the old woman selling flowers
in *Los Portales* looked my way.
If I was for one moment
unfamiliar to myself, then the dress,
being worn, slipped into the cool night.
Whether or not it was a soft breath
of yellow or cream makes no difference.
I can feel it weightless against my wrists.

Chicksha Juvenile Correctional Center, 1980

In the parking lot, there's a woman. Rough blonde shag. Probably a
Texan. Broad in the butt, skin-tight in raw denim. Radio the only light.
Allman Brothers, Lynard Skynard. Coors between her thighs. Outside
the town limits. Beyond the mall and the Tudor-style condos. Almost
the only car in the lot. Light from the radio, green. She would be
his mother. He is looking down from the third floor. Tiny windows.
White glazed brick. It's an early winter. A rare, thin layer of snow. He
is wearing a V-neck hospital gown the color of Scope. Razor welts
on his wrists and forearms. His clothes in a bag in a tall metal locker.
They are running a shower in the open bathroom. His chest is thin.
He is watching his mother in the dark of the parking lot, watching the
snow melt in large cross-hatched patterns on the hood of the Impala.
There are chimes over the loudspeaker as orderlies leave and enter the
floor. Like when you drive into a gas station. The shower. The gray
towels, the attendant with acne. They lead him into the steam of the
large room, his pale skin. His scars bright as birthmarks.
Bright as:

shoeboxes full of Matchbox cars, chicken fried steak, Wichita Tiger's
outfield, the checkout counter at Piggly Wiggly, the hornytoad hole,
his silver Schwinn, his twin brother's body creaking the overhead
bunk, the faintest outline of his mother's nipple beneath her Cowboy's
T-shirt, his beercan bong, the sour Jack on his father's breath, the
bonfire at the company barbeque, his mother's silence, tarantulas
moving over the driveway at dusk, there was the moon shining over
the cars, light from the bonfire on the side of his father's face, the
new redhead receptionist, the gigantic Dr. Pepper bottle at the off-
ramp, his mother's uniform from the Dr. Pepper factory, coupons
tacked on the refrigerator with smiley magnets, boxes of Little Debbie
Nutty Bars, springs busted on the trampoline, the kids fried on meth,
the Merle Norman cosmetics outlet his mom opened in the backyard,

then closed, pecans crunching underfoot, the dead station wagon in the carport, the pole-vaulting championship he missed by half an inch, the rock through the windowpane, his Aunt Jane's forgiveness, the pinkest crape myrtle, brown aluminum siding, there was his father getting in the car with the girl, the light of the bonfire, light on his body and hers in the back seat, holding her head with his big hand, his oily skin, her laughter through the open window, the flat horizon, her widening thighs, the smell of mesquite, looking down at his own hightop Converse, the half-rolled tube of glue, brisket in greasy paper, the laughing, the numbness of his hands as he drew the pocketknife, car motors, the orange sky, the red, the black.

1980. Summer of the stolen Camaro, bandages, Percodan, duffel bags. Cars pulling out of his driveway at night. Pictures gone from the walls. "Thus saith the Lord, the heaven is my throne, and the earth is my footstool: where is the house that ye build unto me? and where is my place of rest?" The Bible left open, his grandmother reading aloud by the fan. His father's fist through the wall. He looks at his arms in the thin streams of water. His mother is in a car in the parking lot. She will wait until he makes a sign from the window. Tonight she will wait there all night. The cold tile. Fluorescent coils. The green gown falling away. She will sit in the light of the dashboard and pick the polish from her nails. He will get out the back of the building and disappear.

Black House

Isle of Mull, Scotland

...every single generation gone.
~Sorley Maclean, "Hallaig"

Atop one corner of a dry-stone cottage
whose three-foot thick walls
bear no roof, I sit the morning
watched by a Highland cow up the glen.
Bracken trembles in a breeze.
Bracken and cow's parsnip choke the two

rooms below me, muffle Gaelic
voices of crofters' ghosts—
Togaidh sinn an seo e—Let us
build it here. Stone laid snugly
and without error on stone, the home rose,
forty-two feet long as I paced it,

turnips cooked over a peat fire,
peat smoke blackened the walls and thatch ceiling.
The roof burned, torched in the Clearances,
these and countless tenants evicted, driven
to Starvation Point, the Mull Poorhouse,
boats for the New World. Two lintels remain,

long stones blessing a window, the door.
Glengorm, a crone replied, asked by the estate's
new owner to name his Victorian castle,
Glengorm—Blue Glen—the owner unsuspecting
blue stood for the smoke of burning thatch.
My boot, seeking purchase to descend,

dislodges one small stone that thumps
down into the corner, a heart beat
in the life of a village.
Wading through bracken, I encounter a thistle
blossoming waist-high, fully spiked
in the doorway between the two rooms,

one housing anger, the other grief.
I pass a windowsill where a harebell
blooms in clumped moss, step outside
this place where I have lived, tenant
for a morning, tourist once again,
the tang of ghost smoke on my tongue.

Repository

With patches the color of darkened blood
where lacquer has not worn off,
with carved folds of your gown hanging
vertically with Cryptomeria grain, and a round
jewel embedded in your forehead,
you stand on a slate platform, above schoolchildren
chattering on their way to see the samurai swords.
Away from the incense and candle smoke

of the temple where you gave your own light,
you bear up under this arid climate,
illuminate a docent's passing comment:
Fine example of a twelfth-century Kannon.
Kannon—*The One Who Hears the Cries
of the World*—Goddess of Mercy,
it has come to this: you
stripped of the supplicant's prayer

and I with my five dollar admission
ticket and a sorrow that has no name,
both of us utterly lost, no return,
no return. Did the temple beams rot,
crack under moss and rain, did vines
grow across the altar? Were you purchased
for a song, transported in the belly
of a B-29? I gaze up at your slitted eyes,

follow your left arm down to the hand,
extended, palm upward, fingers poised
to gather in these heart beats. Who is to say

if either of us is in the wrong place?
We are what we are: you,
carved, wood ears with pendulous lobes,
and I, leaving you to the centuries,
stepping toward the next room.

Van Gogh's Saint-Rémy

"To try to understand the real significance of what the great artists, the serious masters, tell us in their masterpieces, that leads to God."
　　　—*Van Gogh, Borinage, December, 1878*

How what's beautiful blazes—
A drooping star,
An ochre sunflower
Crackling beneath its old glaze.
I stood in your room in Saint-Rémy,
The anguished bed stiff
On its points of lead, the obligatory
Desk as blank as canvas.

The world had already turned.
North light blazed all night
In my rented window.
Stars washed the horizon
Of villa stone.
Those I loved slept, the small fig
Of my heart withering—
As if baptismal, the tears
Unending, the wall of myself
Descending as yours did,
That painted cypress of *The Starry Night*
Kindling funereal
In the foreground of your Holy.

Everywhere, the light
Draws us past stone,
Past the wood shutters the wind flings—
The world carved and delirious
Beyond me, beyond you whom I see
Half listening now
Amidst a concavity of iris,
Of sea swirl,
The poppy mad for such utter destination.

SOLSTICE

The hour, an idea raveling,
a braid accident by wind

or dwarf tornado, snake-
mating weed spawning

the capillaries of high season—
where the clearing ends

into the woods and the woods
don't yet constellate

with fireflies or animal wings
because the filigree of crickets

won't ease, won't splice—
smilax twined in dogwood and

oak, ginger in maple
and sphagnum, lost daffodils,

the greens glow a bit, a skin
of moon, but the only source,

so vibrant, so heavy
on itself, the forest

winks, then goes blind.

CRAZY

Your quilt says *Stay,*
says *Sympathetic,*
though you didn't.
A cabin hemmed with gold
Safe amid the corn.
Says *Mountains help the way*
sure as a hobo chalk
and *Friend* as my friend reads it
as her grandma taught.
Whether you did, says *Rest,*
never hints at *Left behind.*
But I don't say how its sewn
with long, white hairs I've drawn
till its seams wink tangle.
Its lids are shut to cottonseed,
this *Lookout's* pupil,
but not asleep. It holds each ridge
of touch, each warmth,
gives back this heat
no one else can read.
Blooms each moon night
to patch its code, *Come home.*

Call Her: Morning, circling Lake Merritt in Oakland, California and imagining Paris, France

This morning circling Lake Merritt, the birds
rouse the imagination with squawks, honks,
raspy cries. Slick cormorants line log booms
beating wings at mist, clumsy pelicans
slap at the water's sheen, everything
awake on a snake of lake-light crawling
the gnarl of tree trunks—and Angelina
turns beneath her blanket on dewy grass,
turns there to kiss her lover on his cheek
as they rise there, as he calls out her name
like an urge, like a drive, like a hunger.
So in this poem name him Romero,
because you can. Imagine them instead
as they dance lakeside, Bois de Boulogne.

They dance lakeside at Bois de Boulogne
in Paris, France—dance with the same fluster
as birds circling in a raucous laurel
of wing beats, coos. But this is not Paris
but Oakland, California, and they
are homeless where sentries of city doves
preen at water's edge on the lake wall's lip
along a ducky little waterway.
This could be Bastille Day, could be Paris
dressed in pomp and flair, a firecracker
sky flushed in a blush of hoopla. Lovers
are the thing there. If you are not in love,
you will be, or steal into someone else's,
too much Bordeaux too early in the day.

Too much Bordeaux too early in the day,
name them what you will—him Remy, call her
Adeline, because you can. That's the thing
with poetry, it can pose lovers where
imagination wishes to have them
stir or waken or even dance around
in Paris. Here, part of the scenery
and art of invention, her hand in his
rests for now on her grumbling stomach
while a legion of pigeons guards the bank,
feet a polish of pink, eyes golden sequins.
garden varieties, yet necks lustrous
in a royal sheen of purple and green—
but this poem is not one for the birds.

This poem is not one for the birds, but
it is for that homeless girl blanketed
in this Paris of the imagination
wearing a wide-brimmed hat and scented
lavender, not at this man's coarse and thick
hands grabbing mussels young gulls fuss over,
flurry of feathers caught in the brambles,
city doves strutting their velvet nightcoats,
pecking peanut shells she scrambles after.
She dances lakeside, Bois de Boulogne,
too much Bordeaux too early in the day
where a sweet rich napoleon calls her
with strong coffee all the muscle she needs,
someone else busy with birds in Oakland.

Woman Waking, Seaside

The shroud of coastal fog rolls over
a woman lifting herself up

from deep pockets of sleep, from night's
low note still whispering in on the lip

of the wind, on a slow drum of rain.
She rubs the slumber from her eyes,

lifts herself up to the cool wet
of the dawn, while the boats slip in

edging the tombola near Point Sur.
High above a sand spit, trade winds

wrap like scarves at her neck, the day
long and languid stretching itself

ahead, imagination her ear
pressed to the wall of the heavens.

Contributor Notes

Vito Aiuto wrote a book of poems, *Self-Portrait as Jerry Quarry* (New Issues Press). He is a pastor and lives in Brooklyn with his wife Monique. They perform music as The Welcome Wagon (Asthmatic Kitty Records).

Cynthia Arrieu-King is a doctoral student at the University of Cincinnati and an echocardiographer. Her work has appeared in *Prairie Schooner, Margie,* and *Diagram* and is forthcoming in *Hotel Amerika, Court Green* and *Pilot Poetry*. Her chapbook *The Small Anything City* won the Dream Horse Press National Chapbook Competition for 2006 as well as an honorable mention from John Yau in the Vincent Chin Memorial Chapbook Prize.

Jeffery Bahr was appointed a director of MMM sheerly on the strength of the beverage selections he provides at MMM staff meetings. He is also responsible for the formulation of submission rejection slips, as he has the largest collection of them on the Front Range from which to draw on. As he has no formal education in the arts and no experience in literary publishing, MMM decided to grab him before it occurred to the current Administration that he would be perfect as the next Chairman of the National Endowment for the Arts.

Geri Lynn Baumblatt's work has appeared in *American Letters & Commentary, VOLT, the Colorado Review, Elixir* and *Denver Quarterly*. She recently returned to Chicago to remind herself just how brutal midwest winters can be and to write online patient education programs.

Michelle Bitting has work forthcoming or published in *Glimmer Train, Swink, Prairie Schooner, Poetry Daily, Small Spiral Notebook, Nimrod, The Southeast Review, Clackamas Literary Review, Poetry Southeast, Slipstream, Dogwood, Gargoyle, Salt Hill, Pearl* and *Rattle*. She has won the *Glimmer Train, Rock & Sling*—Virginia Brendemuehl Award and *Poets On Parnassus* Poetry Competitions. In January of 2007 she will start an MFA in Poetry at Pacific University, Oregon. Visit http://home.earthlink.net/~verarose/michellebitting/

Sheila Black, MFA from University of Montana, has work in *Copper Nickel, LitPot Review, DMQ Review, Willow Springs, Poet Lore, Ellipsis, Blackbird* and *Puerto Del Sol*. Her first book, "House of Bone" is forthcoming from Custom Words Press in 2007. Her second, "Love/Iraq," was a finalist in the MMM Press Contest. She lives in Las Cruces, NM with her husband and three children.

Beau Boudreaux is a poet and teacher at Tulane University in New Orleans with a chapbook available, *Significant Other.*

Jenn Brown lives contentedly in Greensboro, NC, in the company of shelves (and rogue stacks) of books, a small, mosquito-ridden garden, a beloved boyfriend and family and one canine-fur-production machine. She believes, with Stanley Kunitz, that it is not the life that serves the writing but the writing that serves the life.

Natascha Bruckner is a writer, quilt-maker, artist and student of healing arts. She earned an MFA from Naropa University in Boulder and is currently studying Chinese medicine at Five Branches Institute in Santa Cruz. Perhaps one day these diverse studies will converge in a poetic text on healing. For now, she just enjoys writing for its own sake.

Richard Alan Bunch was born in Honolulu and grew up in the Napa Valley. His works include *Summer Hawk, South by Southwest, Night Blooms* and the play *The Russian River Returns.* Thrice nominated for a Pushcart Prize, his poetry has appeared in *California Quarterly, Poetry Southeast, Oregon Review, Potpourri, Fugue, Owen Wister Review* and the *Hawai'i Review.* His latest poetry collection is *Running for Daybreak* (Mellen Poetry Press).

Cullen Bailey Burns is the author of *Paper Boat* (New Rivers Press, 2003). Her poems have appeared in *The Denver Quarterly, Rattle, Rhino* and others. She lives in Minneapolis and teaches at Century College.

Marcus Cafagña is the author of *The Broken World* (1996), a National Poetry Series winner and *Roman Fever* (2001). His poems have appeared in many journals and anthologies including *Crab Orchard Review, Poets of the New Century* and *The Southern Review.* He teaches in the creative writing program at Missouri State University.

Gerald N. Callahan, Ph.D., is an Associate Professor of Immunology/Public Understanding of Science with appointments in the departments of Pathology and English at Colorado State University. He is the author of 50+ academic articles and two books: *River Odyssey: A Story of the Colorado Plateau* (essays exploring the Colorado River) and *Faith, Madness and Spontaneous Human Combustion* (an examination of the human immune system). His third book, *Infection: The Uninvited Universe* is forthcoming in 2006. He has also published many poems and essays in scientific and literary journals. He has appeared on National Geographic television and ABC national news and won awards for scientific and literary writing and teaching. He lives in Fort Collins, CO with his wife and three dogs.

Susan E. Carlisle has published work in *Agni, Harvard Review* and, most recently, a haiku in *Frogpond*. She teaches writing at Harvard and lives in Brookline, MA.

Julie Chisholm, a graduate of the University of Houston creative writing program, teaches comp and rhetoric at Califirnia State University Maritime in the San Francisco Bay Area.

Julie Choffel's poems are online at *27 Rue de fleures* (www.27rue.com) and *Glitter Pony* (www.glitterponymag.com) and in *The Tiny, American Letters & Commentary, Denver Quarterly* and *Mrs. Maybe*. Julie herself can be found in Oakland, CA., where she has taken up the art of the casserole and the craft of the commuter.

Deborah Gordon Cooper, a hospital/hospice chaplain, is the author of three poetry chapbooks: *Between the Branches, the gods of wild things & Redirection of the Heart*. She and her husband, Joel, a visual artist, live on the shores of Lake Superior and have exhibited their collaborative images throughout the region. www.cooperartpoetry.com

Paola Corso's debut fiction book *Giovanna's 86 Circles* was named "Best Short Stories of 2005" in *The Montserrat Review* and is a John Gardner Fiction Book Award Finalist. She is a NY Foundation for the Arts poetry fellow and author of a book of poems, *Death by Renaissance*. A Pittsburgh native, she currently is a writer-in-resident in Western Connecticut State University's MFA Program.

Anne-Marie Cusac won the MMM Press Poetry Book Prize in 2006 for *Silkie* (see pp. 34–39). Her poetry has appeared in *Poetry, Iowa Review, TriQuarterly, The American Scholar, The Madison Review* and is forthcoming from *Crab Orchard Review*. Her first poetry book, *The Mean Days* (Tia Chucha Press, 2001) won the Posner Book Award from the Council for Wisconsin Writers. A recipient of a Stegner Fellowship at Stanford University and a Wisconsin Arts Board Individual Artist's grant, Cusac was for ten years an editor and investigative reporter for *The Progressive* magazine. Her reporting won several awards, including the prestigious George Polk Award. As of fall 2006, she is a professor in Communications at Roosevelt University and a contributing writer for *The Progressive*.

David J. Daniels has had poems in *Pleiades, Gulf Coast* and *CutBank*. A poetry editor for the online journal, *Born Magazine*, he teaches at University of Denver.

He is president of a GLBT bowling league and leads creative writing workshops for people affected by HIV/AIDS in the Denver area.

Brian Komei Dempster has published in *The Asian Pacific American Journal, Bellingham Review, Crab Orchard Review, Fourteen Hills, Green Mountains Review, Gulf Coast, New England Review, North American Review, Ploughshares, Post Road, Prairie Schooner, Quarterly West* as well as *Asian American Poetry: The Next Generation* (University of Illinois Press, 2004) and *Screaming Monkeys: Critiques of Asian American Images* (Coffee House Press, 2003). He is the editor of *From Our Side of the Fence: Growing Up in America's Concentration Camps* (Kearny Street Workshop, 2001) and teaches at the University of San Francisco.

Sean Thomas Dougherty is the author or editor of ten books of poems and prose including the forthcoming novella *The Blue City* (Marick Press, 2008), *Broken Hallelujahs* (BOA, 2007) and *Nightshift Belonging to Lorca* (Mammoth Books, 2004), a finalist for the 2004 Patterson Poetry Prize. His awards include 2004 and 2006 PA Council on the Arts Fellowships in Poetry and a Penn State Junior Faculty Research Award in Creative Non-Fiction. Poems and prose have appeared in *Agni, Antioch Review, Jubilat, Minnesota Review, Willow Springs* and *The Virginia Quarterly Review*. He teaches all genres in the Creative Writing BFA Program at Penn State Erie and is consulting editor for Penn State Erie's *Lake Effect*.

Ed Downey has taught English at both the high school and college levels. He has a novel making the rounds and another too deep to abandon. He is an acoustic singer/songwriter with four CDs and a member of the Blood and Bone Orchestra (experimental improv), in which he plays reeds and strings.

Laura Esckelson has published in *Beloit Poetry Journal, Chelsea* and *Paragraph*. She was a finalist in *Mid-American Review's* 2005 Fineline competition and recently published photographs in *Calyx*. She is a special education teacher.

Jeff Fearnside, born and raised in Cold War-era Ohio, has lived and worked in post-Soviet Kazakhstan and Kyrgyzstan since June 2002. His stories, poems and essays have appeared or are forthcoming in a number of publications, most recently *Isotope, Permafrost, Rock & Sling* and the anthology *A Life Inspired: Tales of Peace Corps Service*. Currently, he is focused on work set in Central Asia.

Allen C. Fischer brings to poetry a background in business where he was director of marketing for a large corporation. His poems have appeared in *The*

Greensboro Review, Indiana Review, Poetry, Prairie Schooner, Rattle and *River Styx.*

Nancy Gannon has published work in many magazines and journals, including *A Gathering of Tribes, Skidrow Penthouse* and *Fourteen Hills.* When she's not writing, she is the principal of a public school in Brooklyn, NY.

Sherine Elise Gilmour graduated with an MFA in Poetry from New York University. Presently, she is a psychotherapist living and working in Brooklyn. Her poems have been published or are forthcoming in *Isotope, Lumina, Natural Bridge, Patterson Literary Review, River Styx, So To Speak* and other journals.

Stuart Greenhouse's poems have appeared in *Antioch Review, Bellingham Review, Chelsea, Fence, Paris Review* and *Ploughshares.* New poetry is recently out in *Paris Review.* His chapbook, *What Remains,* was chosen for a National Chapbook Fellowship and was published by the Poetry Society of America, December 2005. He lives in Central Jersey with his wife, daughter and son.

Claudia Grinnell, born and raised in Germany, now lives in Louisiana, teaching at University of Louisiana at Monroe. Her poems have appeared in *Kenyon Review, Cream City Review, Exquisite Corpse, Hayden's Ferry Review, Fine Madness, The New Formalist, New Orleans Review* and *Minnesota Review.* Her first full-length poetry book was *Conditions Horizontal* (Missing Consonant Press, 2001). She received the 2000 Southern Women Writers Emerging Poets Award; in 2003, she was a finalist in the Ann Stanford Poetry Prize Competition; and in 2005, she received a Louisiana Division of the Arts Fellowship in Poetry. More poems and art can be found at: http://www.ulm.edu/~grinnell/cc.htm. This poem appeared first in *Alsop Review* online at
http://www.alsopreview.com/thepoets/grinnell/cgunsuitable.html

Myronn Hardy's poetry book, *Approaching the Center,* won the 2002 PEN Oakland/Josephine Miles Award. His poems have appeared in *Ploughshares, Tampa Review, Phoebe* and *Third Coast.* He lives in New York City.

Lee Herrick is the author of *This Many Miles from Desire* (full-length book forthcoming from WordTech Editions, Summer 2007). His poems have been published in *The Haight Ashbury Literary Journal, Berkeley Poetry Review, Hawai'i Pacific Review, The Bloomsbury Review* and in the anthology *Hurricane Blues: How Katrina and Rita Ravaged a Nation,* among others He is the founding editor of *In the Grove* and teaches at Fresno City College in Fresno, California.

Dick Johnson: Born in the Bronx when the Bronx was like Montmartre. Youth in mad country boardinghouse in the Poconos. Army in Germany. To Colorado in time for the Sixties. Influences Ezra Pound and Henry Miller. No books, no prizes, no associates. "The goal is the path and the path is the goal."

Eleanor Kedney is the director of The Writers Studio Tucson program. A graduate of SUNY at Stony Brook, she has been a long-time member of The Writers Studio in New York. She currently teaches creative writing for beginner and experienced writers and poets. Her poems have appeared in *American Poets & Poetry, NY Quarterly* and *Return of Puppy Poetry* (sponsored by Borders Books).

Gene Keller, poet, musician, teacher, lives in El Paso TX. Recent achievements include third place in the 2006 IAMA Songwriter Competition, second place at the 2005 Texas Rasquache Poetry Slam and a 2004 music CD, *EVERY SONG THE MOCKINGBIRD KNOWS*. Keller also has a book of poems, *ONATE AND THE NIGHTBIRDS* (Sun Dance, 1998).

Ruth Moon Kempher, who has called Florida home since 1960, retired from teaching in the Florida State Community College system and from owning a tavern, but she is still busy owning and operating Kings Estate Press, doing more writing—a 26th small collection of poetry was published by Pudding House—keeping house in the woods for two crazy dogs and bowling twice a week, when not travelling.

Robert King's work has appeared in *Missouri Review, Poetry, Shenandoah* and *Northeast.* His full-length book, *Old Man Laughing,* will appear in 2007 from Ghost Road Press. He teaches part-time and writes in Greeley, Colorado, where he directs the Colorado Poets Center (http://colopoets.unco.edu)

Laurie Klein's chapbook, *Bodies of Water, Bodies of Flesh,* won the 2004 Predator Press Chapbook Competition; she recently won the Dorothy Churchill Cappon Essay Prize. Her poems have appeared in: *The Southern Review, New Letters, Mid-American Review* and *Potomac Review.* She is a founding editor of *Rock & Sling: A Journal of Literature, Art and Faith,* where she sponsors the Virginia Brendemuehl Poetry Prize. She is at work on a memoir.

Fredric Koeppel writes about art, books and architecture for *The Commercial Appeal* newspaper in Memphis. He has published a poetry chapbook, *October* (Ion Books/Raccoon, 1987) and a limited-edition artist-designed book *Romance* (Lyra

Press, 1992). He is writer and publisher of www.koeppelonwine.com.

Sandra Kohler's second poetry collection, *The Ceremonies of Longing* (Pitt. Poetry Series, 2003) won the 2002 AWP Award Series. Her poems have appeared recently in *Diner, The Colorado Review, The New Republic and Prairie Schooner.*

Don Kunz, born in Kansas City, MO in 1941. Ph.D. University of Washington, Seattle, 1968. Now a Professor Emeritus, he taught literature, creative writing and film studies at the University of Rhode Island from 1968–2004. His essays, poems and short stories have been in a variety of literary journals. He was nominated for a Pushcart Prize in 2004. Don and his wife currently reside in Bend, Oregon, where he continues to write, volunteer with Habitat for Humanity, hike, mountain bike and XC ski.

Melissa Kwasny is the author of the poetry books, *Thistle* (Lost Horse Press 2006, winner of the Idaho Prize) and *The Archival Birds* (Bear Star Press 2000). She is the editor of *Toward the Open Field: Poets on the Art of Poetry 1800-1950* (Wesleyan, 2004). She lives in western Montana.

Patrick Lawler won the 2nd MMM Poetry Book Contest for *Feeding the Fear of the Earth* (2006), selected by Susan Terris—please visit www.mmminc.org for poems and audio. His other poetry books are *A Drowning Man is Never Tall Enough* (University of Georgia Press) and *reading a burning book* (Basfal Books). He has received NEA, NY State Foundation for the Arts and Constance Saltonstall Foundation for the Arts fellowships. He is an Associate Professor at SUNY College of Environmental Science and Forestry and a Creative Writing professor at Onondoga Community College and LeMoyne College.

Jeffrey Ethan Lee: "I became one of the editors of *Many Mountains Moving* without meaning to. When I left Philadelphia in 2002 to teach in Colorado, I knew only two people in Colorado, one of whom was Naomi Horii, the founder of *MMM*. She published my work in 1997, 2002 and 2003 and my first book, *invisible sister,* in April 2004. But later in 2004 when most of the staff left, some volunteers, including me, stayed to help *MMM* thrive. *Irony:* when "peace valley" was accepted in 2003 for this issue, it was the prologue to *invisible sister,* but the book came out first! *More irony:* thanks to Debra Bokur and Naomi, it was to have been the first work in this issue, but who'd ever believe I didn't put myself first? So I had to change the order! Anyway, my info is always at mmminc.org and identitypapers.org—my 2006 Ghost Road Press book is there now!"

Lynn Levin's most recent collection of poems, *Imaginarium* (Loonfeather Press), was a finalist for ForeWord Magazine's 2005 Book of the Year Award. Garrison Keillor has read Lynn Levin's work on his radio show, The Writer's Almanac and her poems have appeared in *Boulevard, Hunger Mountain, Margie, Tiferet, Per Contra, The Comstock Review*. A seven-time Pushcart Prize nominee, Lynn Levin teaches at Drexel University and at the University of Pennsylvania.

Richard Levine (*A Language Full of Wars and Songs* and *Snapshots from a Battle*) asks: *"In a time of tyranny, how can our writing best express opposition? In a time of war, do we describe the horror or write peace?"*

Lisa Lewis's books are *The Unbeliever* (Brittingham Prize, University of Wisconsin Press) and *Silent Treatment* (National Poetry Series, Penguin). Recent work appears or is forthcoming in *The Journal, Smartish Pace, Crab Orchard Review, Michigan Quarterly Review, Florida Review, SweepingBeauty: Contemporary Women Poets Do Housework* and *Under the Rock Umbrella: Contemporary American Poets 1951-1977*. She directs the creative writing program at Oklahoma State University and serves as poetry editor of the *Cimarron Review*.

Nina Lindsay grew up in Oakland, California, where she now works as a children's librarian. Her first collection of poetry, *Today's Special Dish*, is forthcoming in Spring of 2007 from Sixteen Rivers Press.

David Lunde is a poet and translator whose work has appeared in *Poetry, The Iowa Review, TriQuarterly, Kansas Quarterly, Chelsea, Confrontation, Hawai'i Review, Chicago Review, Seneca Review, Cottonwood, The Literary Review, Renditions, Poetry Northwest* and *Northwest Review*. Most recent books: *Blues for Port City, Heart Transplants & Other Misappropriations, Nightfishing in Great Sky River* and *The Carving of Insects, a translation of Bian Zhilin's collected poems* co-translated with Mary M.Y. Fung.

John S. Mann's poems have appeared in *Alaska Quarterly Review, Massachusetts Review, Fence, Mid-American Review, The Christian Century, The Literary Review, Poetry International, American Letters & Commentary* and *Northwest Review*. He won a 2002 Poetry Fellowship from the Illinois Arts Council. *Mass Destruction, Weapons Of*, a play, was produced by New World Theatre in Goshen, IN.

Frank Matagrano is the author of a chapbook, *There Is Nothing to Love about Los Angeles* (Pudding House Publications, 2006). His poetry has appeared in *Crab*

Orchard Review, Rhino, Spoon River Review and *Cimarron Review,* etc.

Sally Molini has had or will have her work in *32 Poems, Southern Poetry Review, Salt Hill, Calyx, Margie* and *2005 Best New Poets.* She has the MFA from Warren Wilson College and lives in Nebraska.

Ander Monson is the author of the poetry book, *Vacationland* (Tupelo Press, 2005), *Other Electricities* (fiction, Sarabande, 2005) and *Neck Deep and Other Predicaments* (essays, Graywolf, 2007). He lives in Michigan where he edits the magazine *DIAGRAM* and the New Michigan Press.

David Nadal Moolten was born in Boston, MA. in 1961, and his poems have been published or are forthcoming in *Prairie Schooner, The Kenyon Review* and *The Southern Review.* His first book, *Plums & Ashes* (Northeastern University Press, 1994), won the Samuel French Morse Poetry Prize. A physician for the Red Cross, he currently lives in Philadelphia with his wife and two daughters. A new volume, *Especially Then,* was published last fall.

Martin Naparsteck hopes "stupid" is not autobiographical. He's published two novels, a book of short stories and a book of writing advice. Of the 17 people known to have read them, nine said they liked what they read, but they were friends and relatives, so you can't be certain. He is the book reviewer for the *Salt Lake Tribune* and doesn't want anyone in Utah to know he lives in Rochester, NY, because they might take the job away from him.

James Norcliffe, a New Zealand poet, writer and editor, has five collections of poetry, including *Along Blueskin Road* (Canterbury University Press, 2005) and *Villon in Millerton* is forthcoming in 2007 from Auckland University Press. His work in the US has appeared in *The Cincinnati Review, The International Review* and *The MacGuffin.* He is poetry editor for *Takahe Magazine* in NZ.

Alissa Norton has an MFA in Poetry from Colorado State University. A former poetry editor for *Many Mountains Moving,* she is now a soccer, football and baseball mom, freelance writer and sales representative for a quilting and sewing magazine publisher.

Clairr O' Connor: Poet, playwright and novelist, born in Croom, Co Limerick in Ireland, now lives in Dublin. Poetry collections: *When You Need Them* (Salmon 1989) and *Breast* (Astrolabe Press 2004). Novels: *Belonging* (Attic Press 1991) and

Love in Another Room (Marino 1995). Her short stories can be found in several anthologies such as *Best Irish Short Stories* (Phoenix 1996). She is one of the writers included in *The Great Book of Ireland* (1989) and the *Field Day Anthology of Irish Writing* (Irish Women's Writing and Traditions 2002). She has written two stage plays, *The Annulment* (1989) and *Bodies* (1991). Her radio plays including *Getting Ahead, Costing the Coffins, Alma, Artemisia* have been broadcast on BBC Radio 4 England, RTE Ireland and Radio Warsaw, Poland.

Heather Aimee O'Neill teaches literature and creative writing at CUNY Hunter College of New York. Her work has appeared in *Spinning Jenny, Bostonia* and *Ducts.org,* among others. She lives in Brooklyn.

Veronica Patterson published *How to Make a Terrarium* (Cleveland State University, 1987) and *Swan, What Shores?* (NYU Press, 2000), winner of the Colorado Book Award and the Women Writing the West Award. *This Is the Strange Part* was published by Pudding House Publications (chapbook, 2002). She has also published a collection of poetry and photography, *The Bones Remember: A Dialogue, with photographer Ronda Stone* (Stone Graphics Press). Her poems have appeared in *The Southern Poetry Review, The Sun, The Malahat Review, The Indiana Review, Another Chicago Magazine, The Mid-American Review, The Montserrat Review, The Bloomsbury Review, Willow Springs, The Colorado Review, Many Mountains Moving, New Letters, Cimarron Review, The Beloit Poetry Journal, Runes, Pilgrimage* and *Prairie Schooner.* She received Individual Artist's Fellowships from the Colorado Council on the Arts in 1984 and 1997.

Simon Perchik is an attorney whose poems have appeared in *Partisan Review, The New Yorker* and elsewhere. Readers interested in more are invited to read his essay "Magic, Illusion and Other Realities" at www.geocities.com/simonthepoet, which has a complete bibliography.

Emily Pérez teaches English in Seattle, WA. She has her MFA from the University of Houston where she was a poetry editor for *Gulf Coast* and taught with Writers in the Schools. Her recent work has appeared in *DIAGRAM* and *Bat City Review,* and work is forthcoming in *Third Coast.*

Jay Prefontaine has published stories or poems forthcoming in *Quarterly West, Indiana Review, North Dakota Quarterly* and *The Chattahoochee Review.* He teaches writing at Eastern Illinois University and is finishing a novel.

John Pursley III teaches creative writing at the University of Alabama, where he is a poetry editor for *Black Warrior Review*. His recent work appears in *Backwards City Review, DIAGRAM, Poetry International* & *Smartish Pace*.

Karolyn Redoute, MFA from Indiana University-Bloomington, has taught English in Detroit, MI and Keene, NH. She assists students to compose proposals for individualized study in the Inter-College Program at University of Minnesota. She has published in *Telescope, Sing, Heavenly Muse!, Sophie's Wind, Lifeboat, Poetica, Mid-America Poetry Review* and *Earth's Daughters,* and has poems forthcoming in *On the Page* and *Runes*.

Frances Richey's "Nudes and Bathers" first appeared in *The Burning Point* (2004), winner of the White Pine Press Poetry Prize. A Poetry Editor with *Bellevue Literary Review,* she received a World of Voices grant and was nominated for a Pushcart Prize. Her work has appeared in *Cream City Review, Gulf Coast, Notre Dame Review, RIVER STYX, Salmagundi* and others.

Renato Rosaldo began writing poetry as "healing songs" in English and Spanish shortly after a stroke in 1996. He did not expect to become addicted to poetry. His first published poem appeared in *Many Mountains Moving*. His first poetry book, *Prayer to Spider Woman / Rezo a la mujer araña* (2003, Saltillo, Mexico: Icocult) won an American Book Award, 2004. A cultural anthropologist at NYU, he authored *Culture and Truth*.

Ed Schelb's writing has been a long meditation on music and words. His lyrical poetry often centers around music, whether the 15th C. madrigals or the buzz of the mountain dulcimer. His performance poetry focuses on the exploits of Dogbelly, a cross between Greek Tragedy and Texas Swing. He lives in Rochester, New York.

Frances Schenkkan lives in Austin and her poems and short stories have appeared or are scheduled to appear in *Third Coast, Texas Review, the San Antonio Express-News, the Texas Observer* and *the Austin Chronicle*.

Neil Shepard's third poetry book is *This Far from the Source* (Mid-List Press). Poems from the book appear in *Boulevard, Colorado Review, North American Review, Paris Review, Ploughshares* and *TriQuarterly*. He teaches in the BFA writing program at Johnson State College in VT and edits *Green Mountains Review.*.

Sharron Singleton, with degrees from Michigan State University and University of Michigan, has been a social worker and community organizer around issues of peace and civil rights. She has work published or forthcoming in *Spoon River Poetry Review, The Midwest Quarterly, The Sow's Ear Poetry Review, Atlanta Review* and *Snowy Egret.* She was nominated for a Pushcart Prize in 2005. "Beach Stone" appeared in S*ow's Ear Poetry Review.*

Maggie Smith is the author of *Lamp of the Body* (Red Hen Press, 2005) and *Nesting Dolls* (Pudding House, 2005). Poems are forthcoming in *Quarterly West, Gulf Coast, Court Green, the tiny, Massachusetts Review* and elsewhere.

M. L. Smoker belongs to the Assiniboine and Sioux tribes of the Fort Peck Reservation in north-eastern Montana. Her family's home is on Tabexa Wakpa (Frog Creek). She has an MFA from the University of Montana, Missoula, where she received the Richard Hugo Fellowship. A graduate of Pepperdine University and a student at UCLA and University of Colorado, where she was a Battrick Fellow, she published *Another Attempt at Rescue* (Hanging Loose Press, 2005–hangingloosepress.com). Her poems have appeared in *Shenendoah* and *South Dakota Review* and have been translated for *Acoma* – an Italian literary journal published by the University of Rome. She resides in Helena, Montana, where she works for the Office of Public Instruction, in the Indian Education Division.

Barbara Ellen Sorensen is a contributing editor to *Many Mountains Moving* and an editor/writer for *Winds of Change* magazine in Boulder, Colorado. She lives in the mountains outside of Boulder with her husband.

Joseph Sorrentino (cover photographer), who has works on display online at http://www.sorrentinophotography.com/, writes, "I've been a photographer and writer for just under twenty years, beginning both when I was about to turn thirty. A lot of my work as an artist has been concerned with documenting homelessness and poverty in the United States, and I've worked with many organizations, especially those in Philadelphia, where I lived for fourteen years. More recently, I've documented daily life at the Rochester Zen Center, where I've been a member for more than two decades.... I've also begun traveling to Mexico to photograph Day of the Dead, Holy Week, the political situation there and the beauty that is found everywhere down there."

Ira Sukrungruang is a first generation Thai-American born and raised in Chicago. His work has appeared in *Witness, North American Review, Another Chicago*

Magazine, and numerous other literary journals. He coedited *What Are You Looking At? The First Fat Fiction Anthology* (Harvest Books 2003) and *Scoot Over, Skinny: The Fat Nonfiction Anthology* (Harvest Books 2005). He teaches creative writing at SUNY Oswego and is a 2005 New York Foundation for the Arts Fellow in Creative Nonfiction.

Alice Templeton lives in Berkeley, CA., and teaches creative writing and lit at the Art Institute of California-San Francisco. Her poems have been in *Poetry, The American Voice, 88,* and *Puerto del Sol.* She is also a songwriter and the author of a study of Adrienne Rich's poetics, *The Dream and the Dialogue* (University of Tennessee Press, 1994).

Ryan G. Van Cleave's recent poetry books include *The Magical Breasts of Britney Spears* (Red Hen Press, 2006) and a creative writing textbook, *Behind the Short Story: From First to Final Draft* (Allyn & Bacon/Longman, 2006). He teaches creative writing and literature at Clemson University.

Barbara Van Noord of Amherst, MA, has won four Hopwood Awards from the University of Michigan for poetry and stories. She has published in *The American Scholar, Alaska Quarterly Review, Kalliope, Nimrod, the minnesota review, The Seattle Review, Spoon River Poetry Review, Poem,* and *The Worcester Review.* She is also the author of a full-length poetry book, *The Three Hands of God* (Amherst Writers and Artists Press).

G.C. Waldrep has published a book of poetry, *Goldbeater's Skin* (Colorado Prize, 2003) and *Disclamor* (BOA Editions) is forthcoming 2007.

Laura Weaver has worked in the arts, education and social service. She serves as the Program Director of the PassageWays Institute, a non-profit dedicated to nourishing the inner life of students through school based rites of passage programs. She has taught college English and has an M.A. in English/Creative Writing from the University of Colorado Boulder. Her work has appeared in *Prairie Schooner, Hayden's Ferry Review, Rattle,* and *The Bellingham Review.*

Danae Weimer lives in a beach cottage in Montecito, CA. while pursuing a Ph.D. in Depth Psychology at Pacifica Graduate Institute. Her work, deeply connected to creativity and transformation is documented in the manuscript (unpublished) "Naming The Other: The Creative Imaginal Descent." She is the author of *Moving Bodies* from SUN/Gemini Press.

Rynn Williams's collection, *Adonis Garage,* won the 2004 Prairie Schooner Book Award for Poetry, and was published by the University of Nebraska Press. Her poems have appeared in *The Nation, Field, New York Quarterly,* and *The Massachusetts Review* among other magazines. The recipient of a fellowship from the New York Foundation for the Arts, she is a tutor in creative writing in the McGhee Division of NYU. She lives in Brooklyn.

John Willson has received the Pushcart Prize and awards from the Academy of American Poets, the Pacific Northwest Writers Conference, the Artist Trust of Washington and the King County Arts Commission. Blue Begonia Press published his chapbook, *The Son We Had.* An essay on one of his poems appears in the anthology *Spreading the Word: Editors on Poetry,* and three of his poems are forthcoming in the anthology *Under Our Skin: Literature of Breast Cancer.* A two-time finalist in the National Poetry Series, he lives on Bainbridge Island, Washington, where he is a poetry instructor and a bookseller at an independent bookstore.

Kathryn Winograd won the 2003 Colorado Book Award in Poetry for *Air Into Breath* (Ashland Poetry Press). She is a faculty member at Arapahoe Community College and coordinator of ACC's Writers Studio.

Jake Adam York lives and works in Denver where he produces *Copper Nickel* with his students at the University of Colorado at Denver and Health Sciences Center. He is the author of *Murder Ballads* (Elixir Press, 2005), and he has recently completed a new manuscript, part of which will appear as a chapbook entitled *Murmur,* from Poetry West in the coming months. His recent work appears in *Blackbird, H_NGM_N* and *Third Coast.*

Andrena Zawinski, born and raised in Pittsburgh, PA, lives and teaches in Oakland, CA. Her work appears widely online and in print, and she is Features Editor at PoetryMagazine.com.

cimarron review

Subscription Rates

$24 per year ($28 outside USA)
$48 for two years ($55 outside USA)
$65 for three years ($72 outside USA)
Single Issues: $7.00 ($10.00 outside USA)

Submission Guidelines

Accepts submissions year round in Poetry, Fiction, and Non-Fiction

Simultaneous Submissions Welcome

205 Morrill Hall • Oklahoma State University • Stillwater, OK 74078
cimarronreview@yahoo.com • http://cimarronreview.okstate.edu

About Yusef Komunyakaa

the MMM Press Poetry Book Contest Judge

§ §

Komunyakaa's numerous poetry books include *Pleasure Dome: New & Collected Poems, 1975-1999* (Wesleyan University Press, 2001); *Talking Dirty to the Gods* (2000); *Thieves of Paradise* (1998), which was a finalist for the National Book Critics Circle Award; *Neon Vernacular: New & Selected Poems 1977-1989* (1994), for which he received the Pulitzer Prize and the Kingsley Tufts Poetry Award; *Magic City* (1992); *Dien Cai Dau* (1988), which won The Dark Room Poetry Prize; *I Apologize for the Eyes in My Head* (1986), winner of the San Francisco Poetry Center Award; and *Copacetic* (1984).

Komunyakaa has also published prose, which is collected in *Blues Notes: Essays, Interviews & Commentaries* (University of Michigan Press, 2000). He also co-edited *The Jazz Poetry Anthology* (with J. A. Sascha Feinstein, 1991) and co-translated *The Insomnia of Fire* by Nguyen Quang Thieu (with Martha Collins, 1995). His honors include the William Faulkner Prize from the Uni-versité de Rennes, the Thomas Forcade Award, the Hanes Poetry Prize, fellowships from the Fine Arts Work Center in Provincetown, the Louisiana Arts Council, and the National Endowment for the Arts, and the Bronze Star for his service in Vietnam, where he served as a correspondent and managing editor of *The Southern Cross*. In 1999 he was elected a Chancellor of The Academy of American Poets.

Currently a professor in the Council of Humanities and Creative Writing Program at Princeton University, he has been appointed this year as the Distinguished Senior Poet on the faculty of New York University's Graduate Creative Writing Program, which includes E. L. Doctorow, Paule Marshall, Sharon Olds, Breyten Breytenbach, and Philip Levine.

•

Visit www.poets.org for poems, prose, audio and more information about Yusef Komunyakaa.

Many Mountains Moving Press Poetry Book Contest Guidelines

§ §

Prize: The winner receives $500 and publication by MMM Press in 2008.

Submission Period: December 1, 2006–May 1, 2007 (postmark).

Entry fee: $20 {*Entitles entrants to a free back issue and discounts on MMM Subscriptions and any of the MMM Press Books*}

Final Judge: Yusef Komunyakaa

Eligibility:
• Open to all poets and writers whose work is in English.
• Staff and their family members are **not** eligible to enter.
• Simultaneous submissions are allowed if the poet agrees to notify MMM
  Press of acceptance elsewhere.
• Entries may not be previously published, but individual poems and
  chapbook-length sections may have been if the previous publisher
  gives permission to reprint. (More than half of the ms. may not have
  been published as a collection.)

Submission Checklist:
• A typed ms. of 50–100 pages of original poetry, single- or double-spaced.
  (The author's name must NOT appear anywhere on the ms.)
• A cover letter with the title of the collection, a brief bio, your name,
  address, phone number, and e-mail address(es).
• Acknowledgments may be included in the ms. but are not required.
• A $20 check or money order payable to Many Mountains Moving Press.
• An SASE for the winner announcement. Mss. will not be returned.

Send to:
Many Mountains Moving Poetry Book Contest
Many Mountains Moving Press
549 Rider Ridge Drive
Longmont, CO 80501

Visit www.mmminc.org for details about the discounts.

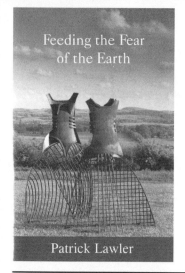

Feeding the Fear of the Earth

Patrick Lawler

MMM Press @ www.mmminc.org

Winner of the 2nd MMM Press Poetry Book Competition
Feeding the Fear of the Earth (2006) ISBN 1-886976-18-X $12.95

"Patrick Lawler's *Feeding the Fear of the Earth* is an outrageously original collection."
—Susan Terris

"Lawler gathers characters as diverse as Christopher Smart, Ed McMahon, and Rosa Parks. Ecological and ethereal, political and historical, philosophical and physical, this astonishing book is a place where anyone who has walked the earth can rub up against anyone else."
—Linda Pennisi, author of *Suddenly, Fruit* and *Seamless*

invisible sister

by jeffrey ethan lee

Finalist in the 1st MMM Press Poetry Book Competition
invisible sister (2004)   ISBN 1-886976-15-5 $11.95

"In these poems Jeffrey Ethan Lee comes to hold and know the whole fragile, euphoric world. *"I could've been anyone,"* he writes, and with gorgeous, insistent and astonishingly musical lines, he moves in and out of selves and what is to be apprehended. This is no *sotto voce* debut, but a full-voiced one."
—A.V. Christie, National Poetry Series Winner

"The title poem [is] a tour de force of persona and plot as a brother watches his sister career out of control.... Lee's careful line breaks and deft use of white space and text, suggest a deliberate and thoughtful architecture. There is much to be admired in all of Lee's poetic personas and voices...."
—Denise Duhamel for *American Book Review*

They Sing at Midnight
Poems by
Alison Stone

Winner of the 1st MMM Press Poetry Book Competition
They Sing at Midnight (2003)   ISBN 1-886976-14-7 $12.95

"If you're not careful, Alison Stone will devour you.... with a voice both edgy and generous, and dozens of surprises that kept me interested and eager for more. In poem after poem the heart-intelligent energy transference from writer to reader happened and happened fully."
—Thom Ward, contest judge

Stone was awarded the Frederick Boch Prize by *Poetry* and the Madeline Sadin Award by *New York Quarterly*. Her work has been published in *Paris Review, Poetry, Ploughshares,* and many others.

Visit www.mmminc.org for sample poems, audio, reviews, events & more. Also on sale at www.spdbooks.org.